How to Engage and Support
Multilingual Learners in
Any Classroom

THE
BOOST
PLAYBOOK

Donita Grissom, PhD
Debbie Simões, MEd
Amy Aglio, EdS
Leslie Mendez, EdD

ISBN paperback 978-1-965438-11-4
ISBN ebook 978-1-965438-12-1

Published by Soro Publishing

For more information about our books and authors,
visit our website: www.soropublishing.com.

This book is produced by Best Questers, a professional development organization committed to enhancing lives in practical, meaningful, and transformative ways. This book equips teachers, administrators, classroom assistants, and volunteers with essential tools to support multilingual learners in mastering both the language of classroom content and English proficiency. By integrating these strategies, educators can empower students to thrive academically while achieving grade-level success and with minimal extra preparation time.

Endorsements

When I was just a young lad, I believe I was in the fifth grade, I knew I wanted to be an educator when I grew up because I was enthralled with learning and loved everything about the education environment. Never once did I look back. What I did not realize at that time was the difficulty with which multilingual learners grow in their content areas. After over a quarter of a century in the field, I can tell you the struggle is real.

I have sat and participated in more professional development trainings than I care to remember. For the most part, those countless hours of rehashed, rebranded theories on learning were typically aimed at the broader student population, with a cursory nod to multilingual learners. As a classroom teacher, I did the best I could, but always felt I was leaving some of my students in the proverbial 'dust.'

The BOOST Playbook should have a place on every educator's desk. The material and rationale that are offered here are invaluable. The organization, thoughtful presentation, and yes, even the use of AI, immediately found a hearty welcome with this reader. It will help the novice to the seasoned pro in nurturing and bringing along your students who wrestle with even the simplest of concepts. The beautiful thing is, the strategies found in *The BOOST Playbook* can be applied and used in any classroom with any group of students. I have always been a content teacher. As such, I have more material I need to convey to my students than I could possibly cover in a year and often feel I cannot give any more time to other things. What *The BOOST Playbook* offers is not an addition to your lesson plan, but rather it offers numerous ways of 'repackaging' your content so that *all* students can learn. And isn't that what we all want? (Be sure to check out the Bonus Material. Such valuable resources.) Growing up is a hard enough road; learning should not be an obstacle on that journey."

—**Dr. Max Shelnut,** Contra Costa Christian High School, Walnut Creek, CA

The BOOST Playbook is a timely, transformative resource that speaks directly to the heart of what educators have long known: effective support for multilingual learners isn't about adding more checklists—it's about aligning proven strategies to meet evolving student needs. This book doesn't just offer tools; it affirms teacher wisdom while elevating it with clarity, purpose, and innovation.

From its thoughtful organization to its solutions-based structure, every detail is meticulously crafted. The authors outline real-world challenges faced by multilingual learners and their teachers, then pair them with actionable strategies that remove guesswork and foster confidence. The integration of AI tools is authentic and no gimmicks, just practical enhancements that amplify impact without overwhelming educators.

What truly sets *The BOOST Playbook* apart is its fusion of research-based pedagogy with cutting-edge technology. It's not just a guide—it's a bridge between what works and what's next. This makes it indispensable for Professional Learning Communities, where collaborative planning and student progress are front and center.

District leaders and school administrators will find it especially valuable for shaping scope and sequence decisions, designing inclusive curricula, and driving equity-focused change. Whether you're a classroom teacher, instructional coach, or system-level strategist, *The BOOST Playbook* deserves a permanent spot on your professional shelf and a seat at every table where student success is being designed.

—**Belinda Reyes,** Ed.D., Chief Executive Officer
Reyes Executive Coaching and Leadership Solutions, LLC
(Former Assistant Superintendent and Executive Director for Multicultural Curriculum, Instruction, and Compliance)

As a language arts professor, this innovative and groundbreaking work has it all. For me, *The BOOST Playbook: How to Engage and Support Multilingual Learners in Any Classroom* uniquely brings a wealth of knowledge and skills with smart literacy solutions for MLs, ELLs, and, really, for ALL students. Each chapter houses a practical and authentic strategy that offers an accessible, research-based solution to a daily classroom challenge relevant to all grade levels. The comprehensive and straightforward nature of this book will appeal to all K–12 inservice and preservice educators who will appreciate the specific step-by-step walkthroughs, the encouraging pro-tips, and the well-organized means of differentiation to benefit all students and their families. *The BOOST Playbook* certainly taps into the positive power and creative potential of supporting students in their vocabulary, writing, and reading growth in ways that are truly inspirational and absolutely joyful.

—**Sherron Killingsworth Roberts,** EdD, Professor of Language Arts and Literacy Education, University of Central Florida, and Associate Editor, *Early Childhood Education Journal*

Often these populations of learners and teachers are overlooked. With today's funding cuts it is even more imperative that school systems have resources for multilingual teachers and students. Finally, a resource was created with teachers and students in mind. *The BOOST Playbook* is your go-to guide for engaging and supporting multilingual learners in any classroom. Packed with ready-to-use strategies, this resource blends easy creative, low-prep activities with research-backed practices to help every student thrive. This innovative book helps teachers incorporate resources that drive student engagement and do not require a total reworking of already developed lessons the teacher has spent time creating. With a playful tone and practical tools like vocabulary stations, flashcard hacks, and formative assessments, educators will find inspiration and efficiency on every page. This step-by-step process to utilize AI is amazing and is easily understood by the most novice of users. This book makes you want to keep on reading while fostering excitement for all of the possibilities. It has the perfect way of delivering content for complete understanding without feeling overwhelmed. Whether you're a new teacher or a seasoned pro, BOOST equips you to create an inclusive, achievement-driven learning environment—where multilingual learners don't just participate, they excel.

—**Dr. Viki Kelchner,** LPCS, LPC, NCC, CSC
James Madison University

The Boost Playbook is a powerful tool for new and seasoned teachers to help bridge the gap between language acquisition and content mastery. It's an excellent resource that focuses on helping multilingual learners to progress to higher levels of proficiency with minimal preparation time and making instruction an easy process.

The authors were very skillful to present steps and strategies that engage students in the learning process, so they can learn independently. Each chapter contains an easy-to-follow format that can be easily used to provide complex instruction, streamlining lesson planning and providing teachers with a road map to help multilingual learners to reach academic success. This guide can be navigated by topics. These range from setting up the classroom, differentiating instruction, using effective reading, writing, and assessment strategies, using games, integrating technology, and much more.

All in all, *The Boost Playbook* is a practical guide that empowers teachers to address the road-blocks that MLs face to reach higher levels of language and content learning. Its strategies and easy, effective planning are all one guide. *The Boost Playbook* contains tools to boost both teacher and student confidence in the teaching/learning process with the goal of reaching higher levels of academic success."

—**Yvonne R. Cadiz,** ESOL and Dual Language Consultant, Yvonne Cadiz Consulting, L.L.C.

The BOOST Playbook is exactly the kind of no-fluff, high-impact support teachers deserve. It treats multilingual learners like the capable students they are—and teachers as the professionals who understand teaching and learning—by offering ready-to-use 'moves' that boost comprehension, engagement, and confidence without swallowing your prep time. I love that it doesn't romanticise the job; it understands the messy, fast-moving reality of a school day and still hands you practical scaffolds, clear examples across grade bands, and smart ways to monitor progress so students level up while you keep your sanity. Whether you're new to ML instruction or deep in the trenches, this guide bridges language and content, normalises differentiation, and builds belonging—all while reducing cognitive load for the adult in the room. It's research-informed, classroom-tested, and refreshingly humane. In a system that keeps piling on demands, resources like this help us work smarter, not harder—and that's how we protect our energy and unlock student success.

—**Daniela Falecki**, Founder of Teacher Wellbeing, www.teacher-wellbeing.com.au

The Boost Playbook: How to Engage and Support Learners in Any Classroom is a must-have for all educators of all subjects and grade levels who teach Multilingual Learners (MLS). This book provides educators the tools to equip their students with the strategies they need to not only acquire the language, but also to master the subject content at any proficiency levels through what the authors of this book call "Moves". These "Moves" are designed to boost comprehension, engagement and confidence in students while unlocking new skills, break down language barriers as they achieve academic success. Meanwhile teachers' preparation time and planning will reduce, giving them the time needed to adjust instruction and address students needs. There is no doubt that teachers of all levels and subjects, as well as all Multicultural Learners (MLS) will benefit from what this book has to offer.

—**Juanita Pérez,** MSEd, Retired Teacher, Florida
Seminole County, Florida Public Schools

I enjoyed reading *The BOOST Playbook!* As a third-year teacher working with students with special needs and specific learning disabilities—many of whom are English Language Learners—I found the strategies especially valuable. Being able to scaffold for multiple learners is extremely important as a teacher, no matter what your student population looks like. The strategies in this book can be applied to many different groups and support all learners across the board.

—Elizabeth Hartsell, Middle School Teacher in Lynn Public Schools, Lynn MA

I'm so excited about The BOOST Playbook! It is a valuable gift and an exceptional resource, providing educators with a practical, research-backed 'game plan' for teaching multilingual learners (MLs).

Its greatest strength lies in meeting teachers at their point of need, whether 'rookie or seasoned,' by transforming complex strategies into manageable, ready-to-use 'moves.' In an environment where teachers often feel overwhelmed with diverse needs and limited training for MLs, this playbook serves as a daily go-to guide. The inclusion of step-by-step walkthroughs, real-world examples, and 'Pro Tips' demonstrates the authors' deep understanding of teachers' needs and limited time. The playful metaphor, from 'powering up' to 'leveling up,' makes strategies feel low-stakes and accessible, empowering teachers to tackle challenges without intimidation.

Beyond its practicality, The BOOST Playbook is rooted in established language acquisition theory, providing teachers a solid foundation that makes the strategies effective. The 'moves' address concepts such as Stephen Krashen's 'affective filter,' using games and low-pressure activities to create an environment that feels safe for all students. 'Comprehensible input' is central to the design, with Leveled Texts and Leveled Questions that adapt to proficiency level. The book also champions capitalizing on students' first language and 'Funds of Knowledge,' aligning with translanguaging theory and culturally responsive teaching.

For teachers who lack formal training, the playbook translates complex ideas into actionable, low-prep strategies that 'bridge the gap between language acquisition and content mastery. I hope this Playbook is a tremendous hit, and I can't wait to share it with my teachers!

—Tracie Carollo, ELA Subject Area Specialist 6-12, World Languages

The BOOST Playbook for English Language Learners is a powerful and uplifting resource that truly embodies a "you can do it" mentality for educators working with multilingual learners. As an ELL Curriculum Facilitator, I appreciate how this playbook strikes a perfect balance between comprehensive guidance and practical usability.

One of its standout features is the low-prep design, which respects teachers' time while still equipping them with high-impact strategies that foster student independence. The playbook acknowledges the developmental differences across elementary, middle, and high school learners, and provides a clear proficiency level table to help educators understand each student's strengths and challenges.

Each chapter is consistently structured, making it easy to navigate and implement. The quick planning checklist is especially helpful for lesson design, and the flexibility it offers—allowing teachers to decide when and how to integrate strategies—makes it adaptable to any classroom setting.

What's particularly exciting is the playbook's forward-thinking approach to technology. It includes guidance on harnessing AI to enhance leveled texts, vocabulary tools, and questioning techniques, all while maintaining a low-pressure environment for language practice.

Overall, The BOOST Playbook is an engaging, confidence-building tool that empowers teachers and supports multilingual learners in meaningful, developmentally appropriate ways. I highly recommend it to educators seeking a thoughtful and effective approach to ELL instruction.

—**Martha Voorhees,** ELL Curriculum Facilitator, Collier County Public Schools Naples, FL

Table of Contents

Introduction

PURPOSE AND VISION:
Power Up Your Teaching, Unlock Student Success

Welcome to *The BOOST Playbook,* your ultimate game plan for helping multilingual learners (MLs) level up in language and content mastery. Just like in a virtual reality game, every student starts at a different level, and your job as the teacher is to equip them with the moves they need to unlock new skills, break down barriers, and achieve academic success.

The **BOOST Playbook Moves** aren't just another set of strategies; they're game-changing moves designed to boost comprehension, engagement, and confidence. These ready-to-use moves can help MLs progress through their learning quest without requiring hours of teacher prep. Yes, these moves will make your job easier and your instruction more effective! Whether you're working with newcomers or advanced MLs, these adaptable strategies can help you meet them where they are and power up to the next level.

OUR MISSION:
Leveling Up MLs in Every Classroom

We've been in the trenches of the education game—teaching, coaching, and training educators globally—and we know the real-world challenges of supporting MLs in content classes. Too often, these students are left playing at a disadvantage, struggling to access grade-level material while developing their English language skills. *The BOOST Playbook* changes that.

With this interactive, flexible approach, you'll have everything you need to do the following:

- **Bridge the gap** between language acquisition and content mastery.
- **Make lessons accessible** for MLs at any proficiency level.
- **Power up student engagement** without overwhelming your prep time.
- **Equip MLs with the strategies** they need to succeed independently.

The BOOST Playbook is your ultimate strategy guide for overcoming the challenges of teaching multilingual learners—from system glitches in instruction to boss-level assessment hurdles. Packed with practical, research-backed tools, this playbook helps teachers with MLs *in any classroom setting* break through instructional barriers, make content crystal clear, and boost language proficiency—all while keeping your workload manageable. Get ready to power up your teaching and turn every lesson into a winning experience for you and your students!

Who Is This Playbook For?

If you're teaching MLs, this playbook is your ultimate power-up! Whether you're a rookie or a seasoned educator, this guide will equip you to take your instruction to the next level and unlock success for multilingual learners.

This game-changing playbook is designed for:

- **K–12 Content Teachers** – Navigating diverse classrooms and searching for next-level strategies to support MLs in every subject.
- **ELL Specialists** – Looking for engaging, practical tools to enhance instruction and make language learning feel like a co-op adventure.
- **International EFL Teachers** – Using content-based instruction and looking for mission-ready tactics to seamlessly integrate language learning.
- **Paraprofessionals and Volunteers** – Supporting MLs in content classes and needing plug-and-play techniques that work across different skill levels.
- **District and School Administrators** – Seeking high-impact, effective solutions to support MLs and equip teachers with classroom-tested strategies.
- **Pre-Service Teachers** – Preparing to jump into the game at the university level and collect pro tips before stepping into the classroom.

CHALLENGES FACED BY MLS AND K–12 TEACHERS OF MLS:
The BOOST Playbook Solutions

Teachers, you are the real MVPs of the classroom, and we see you. We know the challenges you and your multilingual students face every day: low engagement, language barriers, and the constant quest to keep learning exciting and accessible. That's why we created *The BOOST Playbook*! Before we dive into the strategies, let's talk about the obstacles to language learning. Getting clear on these challenges is the first step in leveling up your teaching game.

Every multilingual learner (ML) steps into the classroom like a new player entering an epic quest—equipped with unique skills and conceptual development but facing tough obstacles along the way. From language barriers to assessment roadblocks and social challenges, MLs must level up their abilities while adapting to a fast-paced, ever-changing learning environment. Without the right support, progress can feel like being stuck in hard mode, making it tougher for students to progress—and leaving them at risk of becoming long-term English learners (LTELs).

The table below highlights the biggest challenges you and your MLs likely face in K–12 classrooms and how *The BOOST Playbook* addresses them, empowering your MLs to reach their full potential.

B - Bridges Language and Cultural Gaps

O - Optimizes Professional & Learning Support

O - Offers Ready-to-Use Scaffolds & Differentiation

S - Supports Progress Monitoring

T - Tackles Barriers to Engagement & Belonging

THE BOOST PLAYBOOK:
Challenges and Solutions

The BOOST Playbook Functions	Challenges for MLs	Challenges for Teachers	The BOOST Playbook Solutions
B - Bridges Language and Cultural Gaps	Struggle to understand academic language and content-specific terms, while adapting to new communication styles, educational and cultural norms (Salgado et al., 2024; Kerekes et al., 2021).	Struggle to find effective strategies to make content accessible and engage MLs. Struggle communicating because of cultural and linguistic differences (Saltagado et al. 2024; Freeman & Crawford, 2023).	Provides cultural connection strategies, scaffolded language supports, peer learning opportunities, and meaningful activities to enhance comprehension, communication, and validation of cultural identities (Fenner, Snyder, & Gregoire-Smith, 2024).
O - Optimizes Professional Learning & Support	Struggle to access rigorous instruction without language support, resulting in frustration, disengagement, and isolation (Education First, 2024; Kerekes et al., 2021).	Struggle to scaffold lessons for MLs due to limited training, resources, and increased planning demands (McAllister, 2022).	Provides research-based strategies, scaffolding, and practical tools to build language skills and make content accessible, with classroom examples and differentiation to support all teachers (Support-Ed, 2025).
O - Offers Ready-to-Use Scaffolds & Differentiation	Struggle to grasp grade-level content and assessments without scaffolds aligned to their proficiency level, often leading to frustration and disengagement (Huynh, 2023; SAGE Publications, 2024; Language Magazine, 2024; WestEd, 2024).	Struggle without scaffolded materials aligned to language proficiency levels, often creating their own resources, adding to their workload (Comprehensive Center Network, 2023; Mitchell, 2023).	Provides twelve strategic moves to scaffold content, instruction, and assessment for MLs—reducing language barriers, supporting success, and easing teacher workload (Fenner, Snyder, & Gregoire-Smith, 2024).

The BOOST Playbook Functions	Challenges for MLs	Challenges for Teachers	The BOOST Playbook Solutions
S - Supports Progress Monitoring	Often lack progress monitoring that reflects content knowledge and language growth, leading to misplaced support and limited opportunities (Fenner, Snyder, & Gregoire-Smith, 2024).	Often lack tools to monitor MLs' language and content progress, making it hard to track growth, give targeted support, and plan effective interventions (Fenner, Snyder, & Gregoire-Smith, 2024).	Provides research-based strategies to monitor language and content mastery, helping teachers adjust instruction in real time and keep MLs engaged with grade-level content (Fenner, Snyder, & Gregoire-Smith, 2024).
T - Tackles Barriers to Engagement & Belonging	Often face stress from learning a new language and content, leading to isolation, low confidence, and disengagement. For newcomers and refugees, trauma can further impact focus and emotional well-being (Education First, 2024; Kerekes et al., 2021; WIDA, 2023; U.S. Department of Education, 2022).	May lack strategies to support MLs' well-being and resilience. Meeting their diverse needs can be overwhelming, especially without training for or experience with teaching MLs. (Taylor & Francis Online, 2024; Fenner, Snyder, & Gregoire-Smith, 2024).	Provides low-prep strategies to create a supportive, engaging environment where MLs feel valued (SupportEd, 2025; Fenner, Snyder, & Gregoire-Smith, 2024).

The BOOST Playbook Moves

The BOOST Playbook Moves aren't just teaching strategies; they're precision tools designed to help MLs thrive. Research-backed, easy to implement, and proven effective, these moves make instruction more engaging, accessible, and impactful. The BOOST Playbook Moves Chart is your go-to guide for selecting the right move at the right time, ensuring you and your students succeed.

- Make content comprehensible across all subjects.

- Reduce teacher workload with efficient, high-impact strategies.
- Boost student engagement by making learning interactive and meaningful.
- Align language growth with academic success for deeper comprehension.
- Leverage social connectedness to accelerate language acquisition.
- Monitor language development and content mastery to help you adjust instruction in real time and better meet students' needs.

The BOOST Moves and Their Definitions

Picture Walk – A pre-reading strategy in which students preview visuals and headings to make predictions and build background knowledge.

Vocabulary Building – A strategy that introduces, practices, and assesses key vocabulary using visuals and context at students' proficiency levels.

Flashcards – A learning activity where one side of a card displays a term or question and the other side shows the definition, translation, or answer.

Matching Activity – A strategy in which students pair items from two groups (e.g., terms and definitions) to build vocabulary and concept connections.

Word Bank Quiz – An activity where students choose answers from a provided word bank to complete sentences in cloze or speaking tasks.

Leveled Text with Simple Meanings – A reading strategy that uses adapted texts with clear explanations of difficult words or phrases based on students' proficiency levels.

Leveled Text – A strategy that adapts reading materials to match multilingual learners' varying proficiency levels for better content access.

Leveled Questions – A questioning technique that uses tailored questions aligned to different proficiency levels for any part of a lesson.

Graphic Organizers – Tools that use simplified text and visuals (e.g., tables, charts, diagrams) to organize and support understanding of key concepts.

Cloze Activity – An activity where students complete fill-in-the-blank sentences using words from a word bank to reinforce vocabulary and content.

Review Games – An engaging strategy using games with leveled review questions to reinforce content understanding in an interactive format.

Reread Leveled Text – A reading strategy that provides entire texts adapted to students' proficiency levels for re-reading exercises to build reading fluency.

LEVELING UP LANGUAGE:
How Proficiency Levels Progress at Any Age

No matter the grade or age, learning a second language follows the same progression—like leveling up in a game. Whether you're a kindergartener or a high school newcomer, you start at Level 1 (Beginner) and work your way up, unlocking new skills along the way (Hartshorne, 2018). But here's the twist: how you level up depends on your brain's stage of development.

YOUNG LEARNERS:
Playful Learning Mode

Young MLs can absorb language naturally, picking up sounds, phrases, and grammar through exposure—like earning points just by playing the game (Hiver et al., 2024). Their brains are wired for implicit learning, meaning they don't need to study grammar rules; they recognize patterns through repetition, interaction, and play (Lichtman, 2016).

OLDER LEARNERS:
Strategy Mode

Older students learn language differently. They're less focused on passive absorption and more on breaking down rules, applying strategies, and using their first language as a guide. Instead of automatic leveling, they unlock new language skills through strategy and problem-solving (Ortega, 2014.).

BOOST MOVES:
Adjusting to the Game's Difficulty Level

The BOOST Playbook Moves work for all ages, but how they're used depends on language complexity at different grade levels.

- **Elementary MLs** need visuals, hands-on activities, and simple sentence structures—like power-ups that help them navigate the game and build confidence.
- **Middle and high school MLs** tackle complex academic language, figurative expressions, and subject-specific vocabulary. They need structured discussions, explicit grammar instruction, and academic writing support to play at a higher difficulty level.

Why BOOST Moves Are a Game-Changer

Every ML is playing the same language-learning game, but their progression depends on development and grade-level demands. Infusing one or more of the BOOST Moves into every lesson ensures students get the right support at the right time, helping them level up proficiency while staying engaged with grade-level content.

Every ML is on their own journey, progressing through different skill levels as they build their language abilities. To master the game, you need to know your players! Check out the **proficiency levels** below to unlock key insights, customize your strategies, and meet MLs right where they are—helping them level up faster and win the learning game!

Reading and Writing Proficiency Table

Proficiency Level	Reading Strengths	Reading Challenges	Writing Strengths	Writing Challenges
Beginner	Recognizes basic print and symbols.	Limited vocabulary, grammar and cultural understanding.	Can copy words and write basic sentences with support.	Limited grammar and understanding of the English alphabet and spelling system.
Intermediate	Understands short texts on familiar topics; identifies main ideas.	Struggles with abstract and academic language and complex vocabulary.	Writes simple paragraphs with basic transitions.	Shows common errors in grammar and sentence structure.
Advanced	Reads and interprets complex texts; understands purpose and meaning.	May misread figurative or technical language.	Writes organized essays and reports with strong grammar.	Shows minor grammar errors with abstract or technical writing.

Listening and Speaking Proficiency Levels

Proficiency Level	Listening Strengths	Listening Challenges	Speaking Strengths	Speaking Challenges
Beginner	Understands common greetings and simple commands.	Limited vocabulary and exposure to hearing spoken English	Uses basic phrases and gestures to communicate needs.	Struggles with sentences and clear pronunciation.
Intermediate	Understands main ideas and follows simple directions.	Struggles with idioms and complex sentences.	Speaks in simple sentences and joins short conversations.	Lacks confidence and makes grammar errors.
Advanced	Understands extended discussions and abstract topics.	Struggle with fast speech, idioms and academic language.	Participates in academic discussions with clear ideas.	May have occasional difficulty with formal or technical terms.

(Adapted from WIDA, 2020)

Integrating *THE BOOST PLAYBOOK* and Moves

The BOOST Playbook is designed to seamlessly fit into your existing instruction without requiring a total lesson redesign. Instead of starting from scratch, you can equip yourself with the right moves and activate them exactly when and where your MLs need them most (SupportEd, 2025). These game-changing tools don't follow a rigid sequence; you get to decide which moves to use, when to use them, and how to weave them throughout your lessons. After all, you're the Game Master in your classroom, and only you can unlock the right strategies to help your MLs progress to the next level. The power is in your hands! The following Boost Playbook Moves Chart will help you choose which move to use in each part of your lesson.

Strategy	Pre-Teach	During Teach	Reteach	Practice	Review	Assessment
Picture Walk	X					
Vocabulary Building	X	X	X	X	X	X
Flashcards				X	X	
Matching Activity			X	X	X	X
Word Bank Quiz			X	X	X	X
Leveled Text with Simple Meanings	X	X	X	X	X	X
Leveled Text	X	X	X	X	X	X
Leveled Questions	X	X	X	X	X	X
Graphic Organizers	X	X	X	X	X	X
Cloze Activity			X	X	X	X
Review Games			X	X	X	
Reread Leveled Text		X	X	X	X	

BOOST MOVES:
Quick Planning Checklist for Teachers

Step 1: Know Your Learners
- Remember the proficiency levels of your MLs! Check Proficiency Level Charts above to see what your MLs need at each level.

Step 2: Spot the Tricky Part
- What part of today's lesson will be hardest for them?
- Vocabulary: Consider academic, content, and difficult words and phrases.
- Directions: Ensure they are clear and straightforward.
- Reading passage or task
- Teacher talk & language needed to interact with peers

Step 3: Use What You Already Have
- What materials can I reuse?
- Have I already taught a BOOST Move students know?
- Can StarTech/artificial intelligence enhance what I already have?

Step 4: Pick Moves (Match the Lesson Stage)
- Where am I in the lesson?
- Before
- During
- After
- Which BOOST Moves match this moment?
- Will StarTech/artificial intelligence assist with the move selected?

Step 5: Keep It Fun, Low Prep, and Full of Connection
- Can I make it a game or cooperative learning experience?
- What StarTech can help me create any missing piece quickly and efficiently?

When you use BOOST Moves that build your MLs' proficiency levels and learn grade-level content, your MLs win! You win when you save time by choosing resources you already have and using StarTech apps that create extra resources your MLs need! You do not have to use all of the BOOST Moves in every lesson or in a certain sequential order. You use the BOOST Moves that support your MLs where they need it the most.

Use the BOOST Moves that will help your MLs be successful in learning the language needed to access grade-level content and require the least amount of teacher prep time as possible!

Classroom Setup and Management

Consider setting up your classroom in cooperative learning groups to enhance engagement, language development, and community-building for MLs. This structure encourages relationship-building, increases listening and speaking opportunities, and creates a supportive space where students can learn from one another. When students work in pairs or small teams, they gain more chances to practice academic language, collaborate on tasks, and build confidence in a low-risk setting. Meanwhile, this setup enables the teacher to move freely between groups, providing targeted support, monitoring progress, and ensuring every student is actively participating and advancing in their language and content learning.

What's Inside?

Welcome to your walkthrough guide for unlocking the full potential of ML instruction! This book is your strategy manual, packed with power-ups that will transform the way you teach MLs in any classroom setting.

Each chapter introduces a BOOST Playbook Move that will help you make content comprehensible, boost language proficiency, and streamline your teaching process.

How Each Chapter Is Set Up

Each chapter in this book follows a consistent, easy-to-navigate format, ensuring you have all the tools and strategies needed to boost success for MLs in any classroom. Here's what you'll find in every chapter:

- **Boost Move Breakdown** – Each chapter opens with an explanation of the Move, why it matters, when it can be used, and how to use it effectively in any lesson.
- **Boost Move Specs** – Next is a detailed description of the Boost Move.
- **Step-by-Step Walk-through** – You get clear, structured steps for applying the BOOST Move systematically and explicitly, at any proficiency level, grade level, or content area.

- 🎮 **Game Mode: Real Classroom Examples** – Theory meets action! You'll see how to bring these moves to life across different content areas for four grade spans (K–2, 3–5, 6–8 and 9–12).
- 🎮 **Pro Tips** – Every chapter includes extra teaching hacks, common pitfalls to avoid, and pro tips to help you level up your instruction and keep your MLs fully engaged!
- 🎮 **StarTech: Your Digital Copilot** – Throughout this book, StarTech, your ultimate virtual assistant, will guide you to maximize digital tools and AI-powered resources, to save you time and make your instruction more effective!
- 🎮 **QR Codes** – Throughout our book, look for QR codes for Bonus Content. You'll find templates, instructional videos, and classroom-tested strategies that you can use immediately!

HARNESSING AI FOR ML INSTRUCTION:
Your Copilot in the Classroom

In the immersive world of education, artificial intelligence (AI) can be your ultimate copilot—helping you navigate complex instruction, streamline lesson planning, and support multilingual learners (MLs) with precision. Think of AI as your in-game guide, unlocking shortcuts, automating routine tasks, and providing you with content appropriate for language proficiency levels, real-time insights, and creative tools. With AI on your side, you can level up your teaching, reclaim your time, and keep your classroom running smoothly and efficiently.

STARTECH TOOLS:
Your Quest Map for Differentiation

Teaching MLs at different proficiency levels can feel like managing multiple quests at once. Each student is on a unique journey, facing language challenges that require customized support. AI helps simplify this process by adapting content and tools to match student levels. Whether your students are at beginning, intermediate, or advanced language proficiency levels, AI helps you plan smarter and personalize instruction to meet them where they are.

AI POWER-UPS:
Why It's Worth Integrating

- **Here's how AI can support your instruction and lighten your workload:**
- Plan lessons and activities faster with leveled texts, vocabulary tools, and questions in minutes.
- Reduce anxiety and promote engagement for MLs by providing structured, low-pressure language practice.
- **AI makes it easy to create and customize BOOST Moves, saving time while meeting the diverse needs of MLs.**

No AI? No Problem

We understand that not every teacher has access to AI tools or may not feel comfortable using them. That's why we've included ready-to-use templates in our Bonus Content to help you build effective resources for your MLs—no tech required.

That said, we encourage you to give AI a try, even just to generate leveled texts at the beginner, intermediate, and advanced WIDA proficiency levels (or whatever proficiency levels you use in your state or country). You can easily copy and paste that content into your templates, saving valuable prep time.

Prefer to skip AI for now? No problem. Use the templates in your PowerPoint presentations, and/or let your students write directly onto printed worksheets. Choose what works best for your teaching style and their learning style. Either way, we're here to support you.

Final Tip

First, let's name your BOT (which stands for your AI robot). Why not choose a name that makes you smile every time you use it? Here at Best Questers, we lovingly call ours Chatty Cathy—a nod to the first talking doll we grew up with—because nothing beats a helper with a little personality and nostalgia! Training your BOT comes with a learning curve, but don't let that scare you.

Like anything new, it takes a little trial and error, but the payoff is huge. AI is not hard to use, and it's designed to save you time, not waste it. If AI gives you odd results, try rewording the prompt. A small tweak can unlock the exact tool you need. In our Appendix at the end of the book, you'll find suggested AI prompts for the BOOST Moves. We've also included Bonus Resources accessible through the QR Code below. We'll continue updating our prompt library and StarTech recommendations on our website so you're always equipped with the latest support. We created these tools with *you* in mind—because busy teachers like you deserve practical, powerful support.

With BOOST and AI combined, you're not just delivering instruction; you're crafting learning experiences that meet every student where they are. Let's level up your classroom together. You're not just teaching; you're strategizing, optimizing, and unlocking the full potential of your MLs while preserving your own energy and time. Level up your classroom, reduce stress, and unlock a smoother, smarter way to teach! Here is a list of recommended apps and AI tools we call StarTech. After each BOOST Move, we will give suggestions of Star Tech tools that are useful for that Move.

For anyone who is on the fence about AI, let's be clear—AI isn't your replacement — it's your ultimate power-up. It's here to unlock the next level *you*—the version your students have been waiting for.

Star Tech	Function
DALL·E by OpenAI	Generates images from text prompts for free, although it may have limitations on the number of free credits you can use per month.
Canva	Offers an AI-based design tool (Canva AI) that helps with image generation and graphic design. It has a free tier with many design options, including templates, images, and AI tools.
WordReference	https://www.wordreference.com; offers word-for-word translations in multiple languages and includes content examples and related terms
Collins Dictionary	https://www.collinsdictionary.com/us/; includes bilingual word-for-word translations in multiple languages.
The Free Dictionary	https://www.thefreedictionary.com/; includes bilingual word-for-word translations in multiple languages.

Star Tech	Function
ChatGPT	Can be used to produce most of the BOOST Moves, with the right prompts (see Appendix for prompts that will make creating resources for MLs at beginner, intermediate and advanced levels easier to produce. **Note:** The free version of ChatGPT gives you a limited number of chats and visuals each day, but you have a few easy options to keep your workflow going. You can create more than one account to give yourself extra chats when you need them; schedule a set amount of time or a specific number of chats per day to stay organized; or upgrade to the paid version to unlock more chats and faster access. Choose the option that works best for you, so you can keep creating and exploring without interruptions!
Quizlet	Offers opportunities for students to hear pronunciation, match words to images, and play games.
Wordwall	Creates flashcard sets, spinning wheels, or memory games
Blooket & Gimkit	Turns vocabulary flashcards into multiplayer quizzes or team games
Kahoot!	Provides an opportunity to flip flashcards, take practice tests, and get AI-powered study suggestions
Diffit	Converts any article, passage, or flashcard content to a target reading level.
MagicSchoolAI	Generates custom vocabulary lists, student-friendly definitions, and even flashcard content aligned to your lesson. Also helps design flashcard-based activities.
Liveworksheets	Designs cloze activities, grades responses and provides feedback to students.
EdPuzzle	Incorporates cloze activities into its quizzes, allowing students to fill in the blanks based on the content they've learned.

Star Tech	Function
Gliffy	Creates flowcharts, Venn diagrams, and organizational charts using AI.
Socrative	Uses AI to help teachers create leveled quizzes and adjust the difficulty of the questions to match different learning levels.
ReadTheory	Automatically provides leveled reading passages followed by comprehension questions that adapt to the student's performance, helping to reinforce learning at their level.
TTS Reader	Converts written text into spoken audio

The AI tools selected were free when researched.

AI evolves rapidly, so please verify before selecting and using.

 **Scan the QR Code for updated AI Tools, Apps, and Suggested AI Prompts.**

Ready to press **START** and unleash your teaching potential?

Picture Walk

BOOST Move Breakdown

BOOST Move	Definition	Why	When
Picture Walk	A pre-reading strategy in which students preview visuals and headings to make predictions and build background knowledge. (Schwartz & Bone, 1995; Duke & Pearson, 2002; Gibbons, 2015; Echevarría, Vogt, & Short, 2017).	*Connects to prior knowledge *Builds vocabulary *Sets purpose for reading *Provides context & linguistic support *Promotes interest & engagement *Improves comprehension *Reduces cognitive load *Encourages MLs to make predictions about content	*Pre-teach

BOOST Move Specs

In *The BOOST Playbook*, Picture Walks are like the game trailers of learning: they spark curiosity and set the stage for success! Picture Walks help MLs connect to their funds of knowledge (the skills and experiences they bring from real life) and build background knowledge (what they already know that helps them unlock new information).

This "pre-game quest" builds vocabulary, sets a purpose for reading, and makes key concepts easier to access—just like scouting the map before a big mission. By predicting what might happen next, students boost their comprehension and confidence, much like a trailer builds excitement before diving into a new game.

Picture Walks also offer low-pressure speaking practice, helping students level up their language skills in a safe, supportive way. They reduce cognitive load by gradually easing students into content, just like a smart game tutorial introduces new moves step-by-step.

Use Picture Walks:

- Before reading (to launch a new "quest")
- When introducing new vocabulary (to "equip new tools")
- During discussions or reteaching (for extra "practice rounds")

It's a powerful strategy for boosting listening, speaking, and understanding through interactive, visual learning—giving every player a strong start!

Step-by-Step Walkthrough

We suggest the teacher, paraprofessional, or volunteer start each part of a lesson with a Picture Walk in the grade-level text. This can be done with the whole group or in small groups.

1. **See the Main Things**
   Look at the most important pictures. These give clues about what the book or text is about.

2. **Point and Say**
   Point to a picture and say what you see.
   Example: "This is a volcano." "They are scientists."

3. **Find New Words**
   Look at big words (headings) and pictures.
   Pick new words to say and repeat with the class.

4. **Ask Easy Questions**
   Ask simple questions such as these:

   - "What do you see?"
   - "What might happen here?"
   - Let students answer with words, gestures, or short sentences.

5. **Make Connections**
   Ask: "Have you seen something like this before?"
   Let students share ideas in pairs or with the group.

6. **Use Their Own Language**
   Let students find familiar words in their home language.
   They can use a bilingual dictionary or word wall to connect meanings. Cognates are also helpful.

7. **Keep It Quick**
   Spend about 5–10 minutes just looking at pictures—no reading yet!

8. **Look Again Later**
   When you start reading, return to the pictures to help students understand the story or content better.

GAME MODE:
Real Classroom Examples

Step	K–2	Grades 3–5	Grades 6–8	Grades 9–12
See the Main Things	Look at pictures in *The Very Hungry Caterpillar* and ask, "What do you think this book is about?"	Show fraction ½, ¼ in the book *Working with Fractions* and ask, "What is this book mostly about?"	Look at the picture of an atom and say: "What do you think this is?"	Look at the picture of a king and say, "This is a picture of a king." Look at a picture of President Obama and say, "This was a president of the United States."
Point and Say	Point and say, "This is an apple." Let students repeat and point.	Point to the number on top of the fraction, and say, "This is a numerator." Point to the bottom number, and say, "This is the denominator."	Point to molecules and say, "This is a molecule. Turn to your partner and say the word 'molecule.'"	Say, "A king is the leader in a monarchy. A president is the leader in a democracy,"
Find New Words	Point out new words such as *cocoon* and *butterfly*. Say them out loud together.	Point out words with pictures from the book. Write new words on the board or screen to start a vocabulary list.	Point out important words with pictures from the book such as *atom*, *molecule*, *cell*, etc. Match words to images when possible. Write words on the board or screen to start a vocabulary list.	Point out words with pictures from the book such as *monarchy*, *democracy*, etc. Write words on the board or screen to start a vocabulary list.

Step	K–2	Grades 3–5	Grades 6–8	Grades 9–12
Ask Easy Questions	Ask questions such as: "What do you see?" or "What might happen next?"	Ask questions such as: "Which number in the fraction 1/3 is the numerator?" or "How many parts are in the fraction 1/4?"	Ask questions such as: "What are molecules made of?"	Ask questions such as: "What kind of leader does the US have?" "What kind of government votes for a president?"
Make Connections	Ask: "Have you seen a caterpillar before?" Use sentence starters for sharing.	Ask: "Have you ever seen a big tree or a forest?" Let students think-pair-share. Use sentence starters for sharing.	Ask: "Does food have molecules?" or "Do clothes have molecules?" Use sentence starters for sharing.	Ask: "What kind of leader does your home country have?" Use sentence starters for sharing.
Use Their Own Language	Let MLs talk in their first language in small groups to help understand new words and ideas.	Let MLs talk in their first language in small groups to help understand new words and ideas.	Let MLs talk in their first language in small groups to help understand new words and ideas.	Let MLs talk in their first language in small groups to help understand new words and ideas.
Keep It Quick	Spend 5–10 minutes exploring pictures without reading and making simple comments to connect to funds of knowledge and build background.	Spend 5–10 minutes exploring pictures without reading and making simple comments to connect to funds of knowledge and build background.	Spend 5–10 minutes exploring pictures without reading and making simple comments to connect to funds of knowledge and build background.	Spend 5–10 minutes exploring pictures without reading and making simple comments to connect to funds of knowledge and build background.
Look Again Later	Use the pictures again during the read-aloud to support vocabulary and meaning. Use a vocabulary code breaker graphic organizer as support.	Refer back to the pictures during reading. Use a vocabulary code breaker graphic organizer as support.	Return to pictures during reading to reinforce understanding. Use a vocabulary code breaker graphic organizer as support.	Use visuals during and after reading to reinforce understanding. Use a vocabulary code breaker graphic organizer as support.

Pro Tips

- Keep teacher-talk simple.
- Rephrase and repeat.
- Use wait time to allow MLs to think before answering. If they don't respond, try rephrasing the question.
- Write vocabulary on the board or screen.
- Use partner talk.
- Use small groups for extra help.

StarTech—Your Digital Copilot

Still need pictures? You can create your own free pictures related to the content you are teaching by using FREE tools such as these:

- **DALL·E by OpenAI:** https://openai.com/index/dall-e-3/
- **Canva:** https://www.canva.com/

The AI tools selected were free when researched.
AI evolves rapidly, so please verify before selecting and using.

Scan QR for more resources on how you adjust their speech for classes that have native English speakers, beginner, intermediate and advanced MLs and the Vocabulary Code Breaker graphic organizer.

Vocabulary Building

BOOST Move Breakdown

Boost Move	Definition	Why	When
Vocabulary Building	A strategy that introduces, practices, and assesses key vocabulary using visuals and context at students' proficiency levels. (Marzano, 2004; Echevarría, Vogt, & Short, 2017; Gibbons, 2015; and (Duke & Pearson, 2002).	*Supports comprehension *Strengthens language development *Boosts confidence and participation	*Pre-teach *During Teach *Reteach *Practice *Review *Assessment

BOOST Move Specs

In *The BOOST Playbook*, teaching key vocabulary is like handing players a power boost before the main quest begins. It gives MLs a head start on understanding, builds confidence, improves comprehension, and powers up long-term language growth by reinforcing word meanings, uses, and contexts.

Unlocking Hidden Power-Ups: First Language Support

Think of a student's first language as their secret strength. When MLs tap into what they already know—like using bilingual glossaries, translations, or home-language discussions—they connect faster, level up memory, and boost language mastery (Wei, & Garcia, 2022).

Leveraging a student's first language isn't a shortcut; it serves as a pathway to second language learning, helping students cross into new worlds of vocabulary and meaning with confidence and momentum. Using concepts known in a first language (L1) as a bridge to a second language (L2) helps learners build on existing mental structures, reducing confusion and anxiety. This practice, also called "translanguaging," turns a learner's full linguistic repertoire into a learning asset rather than a liability. A strong first language isn't just helpful; it's one of the best tools for unlocking success in learning a new language!

Power-Up with Visuals

Vocabulary sticks better when tied to visuals, gestures, real-life examples, or interactive tasks. Just like in games, MLs learn best when they see, do, and try. Use tools such as graphic organizers, role-play, or hands-on activities to help words make sense and stay memorable (Bansal, 2023).

Step-by-Step Walkthrough

1. **Teach the Words Students Need to Understand the Lesson**
   Start with words from the vocabulary list in the Picture Walk.
   Add additional words to this list that you notice your MLs need to understand to comprehend the lesson.

2. **Use the Vocabulary Code Breaker Organizer**
   Have students use the organizer to learn and work with the new words.

3. **Show the Meaning**
   Use pictures,videos,real objects, or drawings.
   Act it out or use hand motions.

4. **Explain and Model in Simple Language**
   Add pictures if there is not a picture in the book.
   Use Star Tech bilingual tools to find translations and simple definitions.

GAME MODE:
Real Classroom Examples

The following Vocabulary Code Breaker column descriptions and directions are as follows:

#	We included the # in this graphic organizer so if the teacher is referring to a word and the ML doesn't understand the word, the teacher can say, "Look at word #2. The word is *root*." Also, the students can add words to their list they do not understand in addition to the key vocabulary words chosen by the teacher.
Page #	If the picture is found in a textbook, the students can write the page number in this organizer for future reference.
Word	This is the word students are learning.
Translation	The students can look up words in a bilingual dictionary or app. For young students, the bilingual aide or teacher can use a translation app to look up the translations to include in the organizer and play the sound, so MLs can hear in their first language.
Simple Definitions	These definitions can be provided by a StarTech app for each proficiency level.
Picture	This column is for pictures that are not in a book. The teacher can find these in a google image search or one of the StarTech apps.

Grades K–2 Example

#	Page #	Word	Translation	Simple Meaning	Picture
1	2	cocoon	**Spanish:** capullo **Vietnamese:** kén	**Beginner:** soft cover for a bug **Intermediate:** a shell for a bug **Advanced:** a protective case for a caterpillar to change	
2	4	wings	alas / cánh	**Beginner:** help fly **Intermediate:** body parts used to fly **Advanced:** flat parts on a butterfly's body used to fly	

Grades 3–5 Example

Beginner

#	Page #	Word	Translation	Simple Meaning	Picture
1	1	**fraction**	**Spanish:** fracción **Vietnamese:** phân số	part of a whole	
2	1	**numerator**	**Spanish:** numerador **Vietnamese:** tử số	how many parts of a whole you have 🍰 =1 part (piece) of cake	Numerator ↘ $\frac{1}{4}$

| 3 | 1 | denominator | **Spanish:** de-nominador

Vietnamese: mẫu số | total number of equal (=) parts in a whole

🍰 🍰 🍰 🍰
4 parts = 1 whole cake 🎂 | $\dfrac{1}{4}$
Denominator |

Intermediate

#	Page #	Word	Translation	Simple Meaning	Picture
1	1	fraction	**Spanish:** fracción **Vietnamese:** phân số	A number that shows how many parts you have out of the total number of equal parts.	
2	1	numerator	**Spanish:** numerador **Vietnamese:** tử số	Top number in a fraction; shows how many parts are being counted.	Numerator $\dfrac{1}{4}$
3	1	denominator	**Spanish:** de-nominador **Vietnamese:** mẫu số	Bottom number in a fraction; shows how many equal parts make the whole.	$\dfrac{1}{4}$ Denominator
4	1	equal	**Spanish:** igual **Vietnamese:** bằng nhau	Same in size or amount (=)	

Advanced

#	Page #	Word	Translation	Simple Meaning	Picture
1	1	fraction	**Spanish:** fracción **Vietnamese:** phân số	A number that represents part of a whole or a set, written as one number over another (numerator over denominator).	
2	1	numerator	**Spanish:** numerador **Vietnamese:** tử số	Number above the line in a fraction that shows how many parts of the whole or group are being used	Numerator $\searrow \dfrac{1}{4}$
3	1	denominator	**Spanish:** de-nominador **Vietnamese:** mẫu số	Number below the line in a fraction that shows the total number of equal parts the whole is divided into.	$\dfrac{1}{4}\nwarrow$ Denominator
4	1	equal	**Spanish:** igual **Vietnamese:** bằng nhau	Having the same size or value (=)	
5	1	divided	**Spanish:** dividido **Vietnamese:** chia	Split into parts or groups	

Grades 6–8 Example

#	Page #	Word	Translation	Simple Meaning	Picture
1	35	**atom**	**Spanish:** átomo **Vietnamese:** nguyên tử	**Beginner:** smallest part of something **Intermediate:** the smallest unit of matter. It makes up solids, liquids, and gases. **Advanced:** the basic unit of matter, made of protons, neutrons, and electrons. It forms the structure of all elements.	◯ atom
2	16	**molecule**	**Spanish:** molécula **Vietnamese:** phân tử	**Beginner:** two or more atoms stuck together **Intermediate:** two or more atoms connected **Advanced:** a group of atoms chemically bonded together	◯◯ molecule

Grades 9–12 Example

#	Page #	Word	Translation	Simple Meaning	Picture
1	89	**monarchy**	**Spanish:** monarquía **Vietnamese:** quân chủ	**Beginner:** king or queen is the leader **Intermediate:** a government ruled by a king or queen **Advanced:** a form of government where a king, queen, or emperor holds power, usually passed down through a family line	

| 2 | 90 | democracy | **Spanish:** democracia

Vietnamese: dân chủ | **Beginner:** People vote for leaders

Intermediate: a government where people vote to choose their leader

Advanced: a form of government in which citizens vote for their leaders and laws. The government's power comes from the people. | |

Pro Tips

- You can create an anchor chart or word wall with students, or a digital slide deck to organize new words.
- Teach students how to use the bilingual dictionary as a skill. Model it!
- If you have a professional or volunteer, they can use a ML's language to help them understand content.
- As your MLs master their level, you can easily move them up to work on the next level. This is one way to level up language proficiency.

StarTech—Your Digital Copilot

A list of free bilingual word for word dictionaries can be found here:

- **WordReference**: https://www.wordreference.com/
- **Collins Dictionary:** https://www.collinsdictionary.com/us/
- **The Free Dictionary**: https://www.thefreedictionary.com/

The AI tools selected were free when researched.
AI evolves rapidly, so please verify before selecting and using.

Scan QR Codes to access the Vocabulary Code Breaker Graphic Organizer Template and examples.

Flashcards

BOOST Move Breakdown

Boost Move	Definition	Why	When
Flashcards	A learning activity where one side of a card displays a term or question and the other side shows the definition, translation, or answer.	*Supports differentiation *Enhances vocabulary retention *Increases student engagement *Builds confidence *Builds long-term memory	*Practice *Review

BOOST Move Specs

Flashcards give MLs a fast, focused way to **power up** vocabulary through active practice and quick reviews (Nation, 2001). They **equip players** with multiple pathways to success, using visuals, example sentences, or native language translations to meet different needs (Schmitt, 2008). They **gamify learning**, turning practice into a series of mini-challenges that keep students engaged, motivated, and ready for the next level (Folse, 2004).

Pairing students for **co-op mode** (verbal practice) or using **audio-enhanced flashcards (such as Quizlet)** boosts speaking and listening confidence, helping them gear up for real-world communication (Echevarría, Vogt, & Short, 2017). The more often players revisit their flashcards, the stronger their **long-term memory** becomes, unlocking higher levels of language proficiency over time (Marzano, 2004). Also, this is fun, and fun matters! When MLs are having fun, it boosts their language learning. When they enjoy the game, they level up faster. Motivation, memory and attention are boosted, unlocking real potential for gains (Shen & Lai, 2023). Making learning fun isn't just a bonus; it's a research-backed strategy for success.

Step-by-Step Walkthrough

1. **Make Flashcards**
   Students can make flashcards, or you can use a Star Tech tool. (See below.)

2. **How to Use Flashcards in Class**

   Independent or Pair Practice

   - Flip & Recall: Flip cards to check meaning.
   - Picture Match: Match the image to the word.
   - Whisper & Pass: Whisper the word before the next student gives meaning.

   Small-Group Activities

   - Guess the Word: Describe the picture, while others guess the word.
   - Draw & Define: Draw, while others guess the word.
   - Sorting Challenge: Sort words into categories.
   - Sentence Builders: Use cards to build sentences.

GAME MODE:
Real Classroom Examples

Flip and Go Pro (Flashcard Game)

(Put the words/simple meanings/pictures/translations in this table, and print this out and fold the paper along the center line for students to use as flashcards.)

Grades K–2

Word	Definition (Beginner / Intermediate / Advanced)
cocoon	**Beginner**: soft cover for a bug **Intermediate:** a shell for a bug **Advanced**: a case where a caterpillar changes
wing	**Beginner**: helps fly **Intermediate**: body parts used to fly **Advanced**: body part that moves to help the butterfly fly

Grades 3–5

Word	Definition (Beginner / Intermediate / Advanced)
fraction	**Beginner:** part of a whole **Intermediate:** tells how many parts you have out of the total number of equal parts. **Advanced:** a number that represents part of a whole or a set, written as one number over another (numerator over denominator).
numerator	**Beginner:** top number in a fraction, how many parts of a whole you have **Intermediate:** top number in a fraction, shows how many parts are being counted **Advanced:** number above the line in a fraction, shows how many parts of the whole or group are being used
denominator	**Beginner:** bottom number, total number of equal (=) parts in a whole **Intermediate:** bottom number in a fraction, shows how many equal parts make the whole **Advanced:** number below the line in a fraction, shows the total number of equal parts the whole is divided into.

Grades 6–8

Vocabulary	Simple Meaning
atom	**Beginner:** smallest part of something **Intermediate:** the smallest unit of matter. It makes up solids, liquids, and gases. **Advanced:** the basic unit of matter, made of protons, neutrons, and electrons. It forms the structure of all elements.
molecule	**Beginner:** two or more atoms stuck together **Intermediate:** two or more atoms connected **Advanced:** a group of atoms chemically bonded together

Grades 9–12

Vocabulary	Simple Meaning
monarchy	**Beginner:** a king or queen is the leader **Intermediate:** a government ruled by a king or queen **Advanced:** a form of government where a king, queen, or emperor holds power, usually passed down through a family line
democracy	**Beginner:** people vote for leaders **Intermediate:** a government where people vote to choose their leader **Advanced:** a form of government in which citizens vote for their leaders and laws. The government's power comes from the people

Pro Tips

Here are additional fun ways to use Flashcards:

- **Velcro Match Wall:** Attach flashcards with Velcro on a board or poster. Have students pull and match word cards to definitions, categories, or pictures.
- **Scratch-Off Flashcards:** Use silver scratch-off stickers or metallic paint. Hide the definition under the sticker for a reveal moment.
- **Trifold Flashcards:** Create trifold flashcards with flaps for the following. Then students open one flap at a time to reveal the info.

  - Word
  - Picture
  - Definition
  - Sentence
  - Translation

- **Vocabulary Stations:** Create stations with different flashcard challenges:

  - Match & Speak
  - Draw & Guess
  - Write a Story Using Three Cards
  - Speed Round: 10 flashcards in 60 seconds

Students rotate every 5–10 minutes.

- **Flashcard Audio Match:** Record yourself or students saying the word and sentence. Students listen and then choose the matching flashcard.

Great for centers or early finishers!

- **Memory Match**: Match the word to an image.
- **Team Showdown:** Have one student give clues, while the team guesses the word.

StarTech—Your Digital Copilot

You can use free online platforms that enable the creation, sharing, and gamification of flashcards:

- **Quizlet:** https://www.quizlet.com
- **Wordwall:** https://wordwall.net/
- **Blooket:** https://www.blooket.com/
- **Kahoot!:** https://kahoot.com/
- **Diffit:** https://web.diffit.me/
- **MagicSchoolAI:** https://www.magicschool.ai/

The AI tools selected were free when researched.
AI evolves rapidly, so please verify before selecting and using.

 **Scan the QR Code to access the FLIP AND GO PRO (Flashcard Game Template) and examples.**

Matching

BOOST Move Breakdown

Boost Move	Definition	Why	When
Matching Activities	A strategy in which students pair items from two groups (e.g., terms and definitions) to build vocabulary and concept connections. (Silverman & Hartranft, 2015).	*Enhances vocabulary retention *Supports differentiation *Creates peer engagement and interaction *Strengthens comprehension *Provides immediate feedback	*Practice *Review *Assessment *Reteach

BOOST Move Specs

Matching activities are like **mini-missions** that sharpen vocabulary and concept knowledge through interactive pairings (Gairns & Redman, 1986). They can be used for **practice rounds** or as **checkpoint assessments** to quickly gauge how far MLs have leveled up their understanding (Nation, 2001).

Matching missions might include **pairing words to definitions, images, sentence starters, or synonyms** (Schmitt, 2008). They can be **customized by difficulty level**, adding visuals or first-language support to make sure every player has the tools they need.

These activities offer a **low-pressure arena** for self-paced review, giving immediate feedback (Echevarría, Vogt, & Short, 2017). Plus, matching promotes **cooperative play**, strengthening speaking and listening skills while making learning feel collaborative, not competitive (Folse, 2004).

Step-by-Step Walkthrough

1. **Choose Words & Definitions**

2. **Create Matching Sets**

- Print out and cut the **Flip and Go Pro Flashcards (from Vocabulary chapter).**
- Have students match the words with definitions in a learning station with a group or independently.
- Create a matching activity on paper using one of our StarTech tools below.

GAME MODE: Real Classroom Examples

Grades K–2

Match the word to its correct definition. Write the number of the word in the blank next to the correct definition.

Beginner

#	Word	#	Definition
1	cocoon		soft cover for a bug
2	wing		part that helps a bug fly

Intermediate

#	Word	#	Definition
1	cocoon		a shell for a bug
2	wing		body parts used to fly

Advanced

#	Word	#	Definition
1	cocoon		a protective case for a caterpillar to change
2	wing		flap parts on a butterfly's body used to fly

Grades 3–5

Directions: Put the number of the word in the box that matches the correct definition with the correct definition.

Beginner

#	Word	#	Definition
1	**numerator**		top number in a fraction; how many parts of a whole you have
2	**denominator**		bottom number; total number of equal (=) parts in a whole

Intermediate

#	Word	#	Definition
1	**numerator**		top number in a fraction that shows how many parts are being counted
2	**denominator**		bottom number in a fraction that shows how many equal parts make the whole

Advanced

#	Word	#	Definition
1	**numerator**		number above the line in a fraction that shows how many parts of the whole or group are being used
2	**denominator**		number below the line in a fraction that shows the total number of equal parts the whole is divided into

Grades 6–8

Directions: Put the number of the word in the box that matches the correct definition.

Beginner

#	Word	#	Definition
1	atom		smallest part of something
2	molecule		two or more atoms stuck together

Intermediate

#	Word	#	Definition
1	atom		An atom is the smallest unit of matter. It makes up solids, liquids, and gases.
2	molecule		A molecule is two or more atoms connected.

Advanced

#	Word	#	Definition
1	atom		An atom is the basic unit of matter, made of protons, neutrons, and electrons. It forms the structure of all elements.
2	molecule		A molecule is a group of atoms chemically bonded together.

Grades 9–12

Directions: Put the number of the word in the box that matches the correct definition.

Beginner

#	Word	#	Definition
1	**monarchy**		A king or queen is the leader.
2	**democracy**		People vote for leaders.

Intermediate

#	Word	#	Definition
1	**monarchy**		a government ruled by a king or queen
2	**democracy**		a government where people vote to choose their leader

Advanced

#	Word	#	Definition
1	**monarchy**		a form of government where a king, queen, or emperor holds power, usually passed down through a family line
2	**democracy**		a form of government in which citizens vote for their leaders and laws. The government's power comes from the people.

Pro Tips

- **Start Small:** Begin with just 4–6 pairs when introducing the activity to keep it manageable.
- **Use Learning Stations:** Set up matching as a self-paced station for review, practice, or early finishers.
- **Rotate Roles:** Have students take turns being the "teacher" who checks or explains the matches.
- **Mix It Up:** Have students match definitions, pictures, sentence stems, or grammar structures—not just vocabulary.

StarTech—Your Digital Copilot

These tools make it easy to create customized matching activities for learning, using AI to enhance engagement and interactivity.

- **Diffit:** https://web.diffit.me/
- **MagicSchoolAI:** https://www.magicschool.ai/

The AI tools selected were free when researched.
AI evolves rapidly, so please verify before selecting and using.

Scan QR Code to access the Match Quest (Matching Assessment Template) and examples.

Word Bank Quiz

BOOST Move Breakdown

Boost Move	Definition	Why	When
Word Bank Quiz	An activity where students choose answers from a provided word bank to complete sentences in cloze or speaking tasks.	*Reduces language barriers in assessment *Enhances comprehension and retention *Supports differentiation *Builds confidence and encourages participation *Improves language processing and application	*Practice *Review *Assessment *Reteach

BOOST Move Specs

Word Bank Quizzes act like **checkpoint missions** that help MLs gear up with the key vocabulary they'll need before facing tougher content challenges (Marzano, 2004). These low-stakes **mini-assessments** give players a chance to test their skills, reinforce word meanings, and track their progress toward leveling up (Nation, 2001; Schmitt, 2008).

Using **sentence completion** and **cloze-style questions** with a word bank provides extra **context clues** and boosts memory retention—just like finding secret hints in a quest (Graves, 2006; Echevarría, Vogt, & Short, 2017). These quizzes also serve as **radar scans**, helping teachers spot which areas may need extra practice or reteaching before advancing to the next level.

By limiting choices to a **targeted word bank**, learners stay focused on making the right moves, strengthening their vocabulary arsenal and boosting long-term memory of key terms and other instrumental vocabulary necessary to understand the content.

Step-by-Step Walkthrough

1. Use the Word Bank Quiz Template (scan QR code below) or one of the StarTech tools to create the Word Bank Quiz, saving valuable prep time!

GAME MODE:
Real Classroom Examples

Write the correct word for each definition in the "Word from Word Bank" column.

Grades K–2

Beginner

Word Bank		
seed	root	

#	Simple Meaning	Word from Word Bank
1	helps the plant stay in the dirt takes water from the dirt	

2	makes a new plant	

Intermediate

Word Bank		
seed	root	

#	Simple Meaning	Word from Word Bank
1	helps the plant stay in the dirt takes water from the dirt	
2	grows into a plant when it gets water and sun	

Advanced

Word Bank		
seed	root	

#	Simple Meaning	Word from Word Bank
1	keeps the plant in the ground and takes in water to help it grow	
2	has a tiny plant inside with water, sun, and soil, it grows into a full plant	

Grades 3–5

Beginner

Word Bank		
numerator	denominator	

#	Simple Meaning	Word from Word Bank
1	top number in a fraction how many parts of a whole you have	
2	bottom number in a fraction total number of equal (=) parts in a whole	

Intermediate

Word Bank		
numerator	denominator	

#	Simple Meaning	Word from Word Bank
1	bottom number in a fraction, shows how many equal parts make the whole	
2	top number in a fraction, shows how many parts are being counted	

Advanced

Word Bank		
numerator	denominator	

#	Simple Meaning	Word from Word Bank
1	number above the line in a fraction, shows how many parts of the whole or group are being used	
2	number below the line in a fraction, shows the total number of equal parts the whole is divided into.	

Grades 6–8

Beginner

Word Bank		
atom	molecule	

#	Simple Meaning	Word from Word Bank
1	the smallest part of something	
2	two or more atoms stuck together	

Intermediate

Word Bank		
atom	molecule	

#	Simple Meaning	Word from Word Bank
1	An atom is the smallest unit of matter. It makes up solids, liquids, and gases.	
2	A molecule is two or more atoms connected.	

Advanced

Word Bank		
atom	molecule	

#	Simple Meaning	Word from Word Bank
1	A molecule is a group of atoms chemically bonded together.	
2	An atom is the basic unit of matter, made of protons, neutrons, and electrons. It forms the structure of all elements.	

Grades 9–12

Beginner

Word Bank		
monarchy	democracy	

#	Simple Meaning	Word from Word Bank
1	A king or queen is the leader.	
2	People vote for leaders	

Intermediate

Word Bank		
monarchy	democracy	

#	Simple Meaning	Word from Word Bank
1	a government ruled by a king or queen	
2	a government where people vote to choose their leader	

Advanced

Word Bank		
monarchy	democracy	

#	Simple Meaning	Word from Word Bank
1	a form of government where a king, queen, or emperor holds power, usually passed down through a family line	
2	a form of government in which citizens vote for their leaders and laws. The government's power comes from the people.	

Pro Tips

- **Differentiate by Level:** Use fewer choices for beginners or give extra clues. For advanced MLs, include more abstract or academic terms.
- **Make It Interactive:** Turn the quiz into a game (e.g., team race) to increase engagement.
- **Leverage Tech Tools:** Use StarTech tools to generate quickly and save prep time.
- **Guided Notes:** Use word banks to help students fill in the blanks or complete partially scaffolded notes.
- **Writing Support:** Offer word banks with sentence starters, transition words, or key vocabulary to support writing tasks.

StarTech—Your Digital Copilot

These tools make it easy to create customized word bank activities for learning, using AI to enhance engagement and interactivity.

- **Quizlet:** https://www.quizlet.com
- **Wordwall:** https://wordwall.net/
- **Blooket:** https://www.blooket.com/
- **Kahoot!:** https://kahoot.com/
- **Diffit:** https://web.diffit.me/
- **MagicSchoolAI:** https://www.magicschool.ai/

The AI tools selected were free when researched.
AI evolves rapidly, so please verify before selecting and using.

Scan QR Code to access the Word Bank Quiz Template and examples.

Leveled Text with Simple Meanings

BOOST Move Breakdown

Boost Move	Definition	Why	When
Simple Meanings	A reading strategy that uses adapted texts with clear explanations of difficult words or phrases based on students' proficiency levels	*Reduces cognitive load *Supports language acquisition *Improves reading fluency *Enhances content understanding	*Pre-teach *During Teach *Practice *Review *Assessments *Re-teach

BOOST Move Specs

Leveled texts with simple meanings are like **access passes** that help multilingual learners (MLs) enter the game at just the right level. These texts include **clear explanations of tricky words**, breaking down complex language so players can stay in the action and keep moving forward (Nutta et al., 2018, 2020).

Providing **simplified definitions** within or alongside the text acts like **bonus hints** or **strategy guides**, keeping learners engaged and boosting their language skills over time (Schleppegrell, 2004; Marzano, 2004; Gibbons, 2015; WIDA, 2023). Instead of hitting frustrating obstacles, players build vocabulary and comprehension steadily, unlocking **new abilities** and reaching higher levels of understanding with each lesson. Also, giving MLs small chunks of text at a time instead of the entire leveled text gives them a better chance of comprehending and learning the content. In other words, baby steps instead of giant leaps!

Chunking Text Is a Game-Changer

Imagine you're starting a brand-new quest in a massive open-world video game. You wouldn't want the entire map, every mission, and all the enemies thrown at you at once, right? Total overload = instant *Game Over*.

For MLs, reading a giant block of text feels the same way. It's like being dropped into the hardest level without a tutorial or a guide. Instead, give them *chunks* of text— small, manageable "missions." It's like offering checkpoints and clear power-ups along the way. Here's why:

- **Focus Mode Activated:** They can concentrate on one idea or skill at a time without getting overwhelmed.
- **Memory Boost:** Smaller sections are easier to digest and remember, equipping them for future challenges.
- **Quick Wins:** Finishing each chunk gives them a sense of accomplishment—just like winning a level!
- **Strategy Time:** After each chunk, players (students) can pause, reflect, and upgrade their skills before moving to the next quest.

By breaking down the full text into smaller quests, we make the whole adventure feel achievable, exciting, and—most importantly—winnable!

Step-by-Step Walkthrough

1. **Select a Chunk of the Text**

    - Go to the grade-level text.
    - Select the text that correlates with the standards/objectives of the lesson.
    - Using one of the StarTech Tools, level that text for your students' WIDA proficiency levels— beginner, intermediate, and/or advanced.
    - Select a chunk of that text to create any of the BOOST moves you decide your MLs need.
    - Work with one chunk of text at a time.

2. **Provide Simple Meanings**

    - For Leveled Text with Simple Meanings, be sure the words or phrases MLs need to know are highlighted or bolded. (You can ask the StarTech to do that if it doesn't already do it for you.)
    - Next, be sure the StarTech gives the Leveled Text in the left column and the simple definitions in the right column, according to WIDA proficiency levels.

GAME MODE:
Real Classroom Examples

Beginner

Text	Definition
A fraction shows part of something.	**Fraction**: a part of a whole
The top number is the numerator. It tells how many parts of a whole you have.	**Numerator**: how many parts of a whole you have

| The bottom number is the denominator. It tells the total number of equal (=) parts in a whole. | **Denominator**: total number of equal (=) parts in a whole |

Intermediate

Text	Definition
A fraction shows a part of a whole. It has two numbers.	**Fraction**: a number that shows how many parts you have out of the total number of equal parts
The numerator (top number) tells how many parts are counted.	**Numerator**: the number that shows how many parts are counted
The denominator (bottom number) tells how many equal parts make the whole.	**Denominator**: the number that shows how many parts make up the whole

Advanced

Text	Definition
Fractions represent parts of a whole that have been divided into equal sections.	**Fraction**: a number that represents part of a whole or a set, written as one number over another (numerator over denominator)
The numerator shows how many parts are being considered.	**Numerator**: number above the line in a fraction, shows how many parts of the whole or group are being used
The denominator shows the total number of equal parts in the whole.	**Denominator**: number below the line in a fraction, shows the total number of equal parts the whole is divided into
Fractions are used in real life when measuring, cooking, dividing objects, and understanding time.	**Real-life use**: Fractions help describe parts of things in everyday life.

Pro Tips

- **Narrate PowerPoints:** Create narrated PowerPoint presentations, and set them up at a learning station for students to access, listening to authentic English speakers, which enhances their language acquisition.
- **Reading Options:** Have students read with a partner or in small groups to improve comprehension.
- **Create Videos for Learning Stations:** Use tools like Screencastify to record videos that students can watch at a learning station.
- **Text-to-Speech Tool:** Copy and paste text into TTS Reader (https://ttsreader.com/), so students can listen to the text at a listening station.

StarTech—Your Digital Copilot

These tools make it easy to create customized leveled activities for learning, using AI to enhance engagement and interactivity.

- **Diffit:** https://web.diffit.me/
- **MagicSchoolAI:** https://www.magicschool.ai/

The AI tools selected were free when researched.
AI evolves rapidly, so please verify before selecting and using.

 *Scan QR Code to access Leveled Text with Simple Meanings.*

Leveled Text

BOOST Move Breakdown

Boost Move	Definition	Why	When
Leveled Text	A strategy that adapts reading materials to match MLs' varying proficiency levels for better content access (Nutta et al., 2018, 2020).	*Supports comprehensible input *Encourages language growth *Increases engagement *Bridges the gap to grade-level content	*Pre-teach *During Teach *Practice *Review *Assessment *Reteach

BOOST Move Specs

Using texts matched to each ML's proficiency level is like giving every player the **perfect starter gear** for their adventure. It grants access to grade-level **quests**, builds vocabulary, and grows confidence with every challenge they conquer (Nutta et al., 2018, 2020; Gibbons, 2015).

Here's why it works:

- **Boosts Comprehension:** Makes the input more understandable and helps them power through early missions (Echevarría, Vogt, & Short, 2017).

- **Supports Scaffolding:** Gradually ramps up text complexity—just like unlocking higher-level gear—so players build academic language and fluency over time (Fountas & Pinnell, 2016; Gibbons, 2015).
- **Encourages Participation:** Ensures every ML can jump into the action, engage meaningfully, and build confidence as an active team member (WIDA, 2023).
- **Differentiates the Journey:** Customizes instruction for mixed-ability classrooms, helping each player grow at their own pace, no matter where they start.

Step-by-Step Walkthrough

1. **Select the Text**
   Choose or create a passage that can be modified for beginner, intermediate, and advanced readers.

2. **Create Leveled Versions**
   Use a StarTech Tool to reduce your teacher prep time to adjust the reading level of the text while keeping the main idea and theme consistent.

GAME MODE:
Real Classroom Examples

Grade and Proficiency Level Examples of Leveled Text

Grades	Leveled Text
Grades K–2 Beginner	He woke up. He was not a caterpillar. He pushed. The cocoon opened. He had wings! The wings were red, blue, yellow and green. He flapped his wings. He went up, up, up! "I can fly!" said the butterfly.

Grades	Leveled Text
Grades K–2 Intermediate	When he woke up, he was not a caterpillar anymore. He pushed and pushed. The cocoon opened. Two wings came out. They were beautiful! He became a butterfly. His wings were red, blue, yellow, and green. He flapped his wings.He flew up into the sky. "I can fly!" said the butterfly.
Grades K–2 Advanced	When he woke up, he was not a caterpillar anymore! He pushed and pushed. The cocoon split (broke open into parts) open. Out came two beautiful wings! He had turned into a colorful butterfly! His wings were red, blue, yellow, and green. He flapped (moved up and down) his new wings. Up, up he flew into the bright blue sky. "I can fly!" said the happy butterfly.
Grades 3–5 Beginner	Numerator = top number in a fraction numerator = how many parts of a whole you have denominator = bottom number in a fraction denominator = how many equal parts in a whole
Grades 3–5 Intermediate	The numerator is the top number in a fraction. It shows how many parts you have. The denominator is the bottom number in a fraction. It tells how many equal parts make up the whole.
Grades 3–5 Advanced	Fractions represent parts of a whole that have been divided into equal sections. Each fraction has two important parts: The numerator (top number) shows how many parts are being considered. The denominator (bottom number) shows the total number of equal parts in the whole. Fractions are used in real life when measuring, cooking, dividing objects, and understanding time.

Grades	Leveled Text
Grades 6–8 Beginner	atom = small piece of matter molecule = two or more atoms stuck together
Grades 6–8 Intermediate	An atom is a small piece of matter. A molecule is two or more atoms stuck together.
Grades 6–8 Advanced	An atom is a small unit of matter that makes up everything around us. A molecule consists of two or more atoms that are bonded together.
Grades 9–12 Beginner	monarchy = king or queen is the leader democracy = people vote to pick leaders
Grades 9–12 Intermediate	A monarchy is a type of government where a king or queen is the leader. In a democracy, the people can vote to choose their leaders.
Grades 9–12 Advanced	A monarchy is a form of government where a king or queen serves as the leader. In contrast, a democracy allows citizens to have the power to vote for their leaders.

Pro Tips

- **Level Up Gradually:** Think of text difficulty like game levels. Start at the learner's current stage and, working within their zone of proximal development—the gap between their current and potential abilities—slowly introduce more complex structures with guidance (Vygotsky, 1978). Celebrate "level-ups" in fluency, comprehension and their willingness to take risks in using the new language!

- **Use Visual Boosts and Context Clues:** Support new texts with images, graphic organizers, and sentence starters. These function like boost items in a game, giving learners extra energy to tackle new content.

- **Keep It Low-Stakes and High-Fun:** Frame leveled text activities as practice runs, not final boss battles. Low-pressure opportunities encourage risk-taking and build confidence over time.

- **Monitor Progress Like a Game Map:** Track small wins—new vocabulary mastered, summaries written, fluency improved—and show students their progress visually with a chart, graph, stickers, or some other way that shows their progress.

StarTech—Your Digital Copilot

These tools make it easy to create customized leveled activities for learning, using AI to enhance engagement and interactivity.

- **ReadTheory: https://readtheory.org/**
- **Diffit:** https://web.diffit.me/
- **MagicSchoolAI:** https://www.magicschool.ai/

The AI tools selected were free when researched.
I evolves rapidly, so please verify before selecting and using.

 *Scan QR Code to access Leveled Text examples.*

"Every tough level is a step closer to greatness—master the difficult steps, and you'll unlock your ultimate achievements!"

Leveled Questions

BOOST Move Breakdown

Boost Move	Definition	Why	When
Leveled Questions	A questioning technique that uses tailored questions aligned to different proficiency levels for any part of a lesson (Nutta et al., 2018, 2020).	*Supports comprehensible input *Scaffolds instruction *Encourages language growth *Encourages critical thinking and problem-solving *Supports both oral and written language development *Lowers affective filter	*Pre-teach *During Teach *Practice *Review *Assessments *Reteach

BOOST Move Specs

Leveled questions are like **mission prompts** that guide players (your brilliant MLs) through different stages of the quest. These **scaffolded challenges** range from basic recall to higher-order critical thinking, supporting content mastery and language development (Zwiers, 2014;

Nutta et al., 2020). Leveled questions turn everyday classroom conversations into **interactive quests**, keeping every player active, thinking, and moving forward.

- **Tailored to Skill Level:**
  Each question is **tailored to the player's current skill level**, starting with simpler prompts and gradually powering up to more complex tasks. This lets MLs participate meaningfully in discussions, assessments, and classroom missions (Gibbons, 2015; WIDA, 2023).
- **Access to Grade-Level Concepts:**
  Learners explore big ideas at a pace that matches their progress (Fountas & Pinnell, 2016).
- **Vocabulary, Critical Thinking, and Communication Power-Ups:**
  Every question boosts academic language, reasoning skills, and expression (Zwiers, 2014; Gibbons, 2015).
- **Stronger Oral and Written Language Skills:**
  Players build up both talking and writing abilities for the challenges ahead.
- **More Language Output and Engagement:**
  Learners stay in the game longer, think harder, and share more ideas (Echevarría, Vogt, & Short, 2017).

Step-by-Step Walkthrough

1. **Create Leveled Questions**

   Start with the questions from the grade-level text or teacher's edition. You can use your own questions, too. Use a StarTech Tool to create beginner, intermediate, and advanced questions for your MLs. This saves you time and makes your prep easier.

2. **When to Use Leveled Questions**

   Use in any portion of a lesson including but not limited to guided reading; practice and review activities; listening, speaking, reading and writing activities; and, in both formative and summative assessments to measure content knowledge and language progress effectively (WIDA, 2023).

3. **Practice Quiz**

   Allow MLs to take a practice quiz using leveled questions at their proficiency level before attempting the grade-level assessment. This is a critical step in acquiring the language necessary to master the content! Having this vital scaffold will give your students a better chance to master the grade level content and be successful and feel more confident and equipped to take the grade-level assessment.

GAME MODE:
Real Classroom Examples

Beginner

Text	Leveled Questions
Igneous rocks = hot melted rock cooling Sedimentary rocks = weathering and erosion pushing small rocks together in layers Metamorphic rocks = very high heat and pressure	What is this? (Point to picture of an igneous rock with the word labeled.) Is this a metamorphic rock? (Yes/No) What is this? (Give either/or choice pointing to labeled images.)

Intermediate

Text	Leveled Questions
Metamorphic rocks are made when a rock is put under a lot of heat and pressure, and it forms a new rock under the Earth's surface.	High heat and (what) make a metamorphic rock? Do metamorphic rocks form above or below (under) the Earth?

Advanced

Text	Leveled Questions
Igneous means fire! Igneous rocks are created deep inside the Earth and made from melted rock. The melted rock is known as magma. Magma is an extremely hot liquid and when it cools it hardens. Magma can cool below the surface of the Earth and also above the surface. If it cools above the surface, it's called lava. Igneous rocks are formed when magma or lava cools and becomes solid.	Why do you think *igneous* means fire? What is the difference between magma and lava? Do you think igneous rocks created from magma look different than the ones created from lava?

Pro Tips

- **Utilize in various settings:** during guided reading, practice sessions, review games, or assessment activities.
- **Use in whole-group or small-group** discussions, or at learning stations to foster engagement and understanding.
- **Use in different settings, such as** guided reading, practice, review games, assessments.
- **Think Aloud:** Model how to break down and answer a question step by step.
- Start with simple questions, and then move to deeper thinking.
- **Add Sentence Frames:** Support responses with structured starters.
- **Use Multiple Modes:** Combine questions with visuals (images, diagrams, or realia), movement, or hands-on tools for clarity.

StarTech—Your Digital Copilot

These tools can be used to create customized and leveled questions, helping educators provide differentiated instruction and ensuring that students are challenged at their appropriate learning levels.

- **Quizlet:** https://www.quizlet.com
- **Kahoot!:** https://kahoot.com/
- **Socrative:** https://www.socrative.com/
- **Edpuzzle:** https://edpuzzle.com/

The AI tools selected were free when researched.
AI evolves rapidly, so please verify before selecting and using.

Scan QR Code to access the Leveled Questions template and examples.

Graphic Organizers

BOOST Move Breakdown

Boost Move	Definition	Why	When
Graphic Organizers	A tool that uses simplified text and visuals (e.g., tables, charts, diagrams) to organize and support understanding of key concepts (Jiang & Grabe, 2007).	*Improves reading comprehension *Enhances writing performance *Enhances critical thinking *Organizes information visually *Makes content more comprehensible *Supports all proficiency levels *Supports language growth *Activates prior knowledge	*Pre-teach *During Teach *Practice *Review *Assessments *Reteach

Boost Move Specs

Graphic organizers are **game maps** that guide MLs through new worlds of information. These visual tools help players **organize details**, **understand complex quests**, and **build powerful academic language** along the way (Nutta et al., 2018, 2022; Rodríguez & Rodríguez, 2020).

Here's why they work:

- **Make Content and Vocabulary More Accessible:** Graphic organizers break down tough ideas into easy-to-follow paths.
- **Improve Comprehension and Memory:** Players remember more when they can **see** how ideas connect—like tracking locations on a quest map.
- **Support Writing Structure and Clarity:** Graphic organizers help players organize thoughts before writing, like setting up a **strategy guide** before a big boss battle.
- **Activate Prior Knowledge and Connect Ideas:** They help players **link past missions** to new ones, boosting understanding and critical thinking.
- **Boost Performance on Assignments and Assessments:** Clear maps mean **fewer wrong turns** and stronger results (Aznan & Saad, 2023; Colorín Colorado, n.d.).

Formats like **charts, diagrams, webs, and mind maps** can be adapted for any subject, any skill level, equipping every learner with the tools they need to win their learning quests.

Step-by-Step Walkthrough

Graphic organizers are simple, powerful tools that help multilingual learners visually organize ideas, boost comprehension, and build critical thinking across all content areas.

1. **Select a Graphic Organize**r:
   Use StarTech Tool to reduce your teacher prep time. Choose one that fits your lesson goal (e.g., Venn diagram, flowchart, T-chart, concept map, KWL chart).

2. **Model:**
   Guide students as they complete the organizer to compare, categorize, outline steps, or track progress. Use individually or in groups. Demonstrate the connection between the text and the organizer.

3. **Discuss:**
   Review completed organizers. Encourage students to find patterns, make connections, and reflect on their learning.

4. **Apply:**
   Use the organizer as a springboard for listening, speaking, reading and/or writing.

GAME MODE:
Real Classroom Examples

Grades 3–5 Example

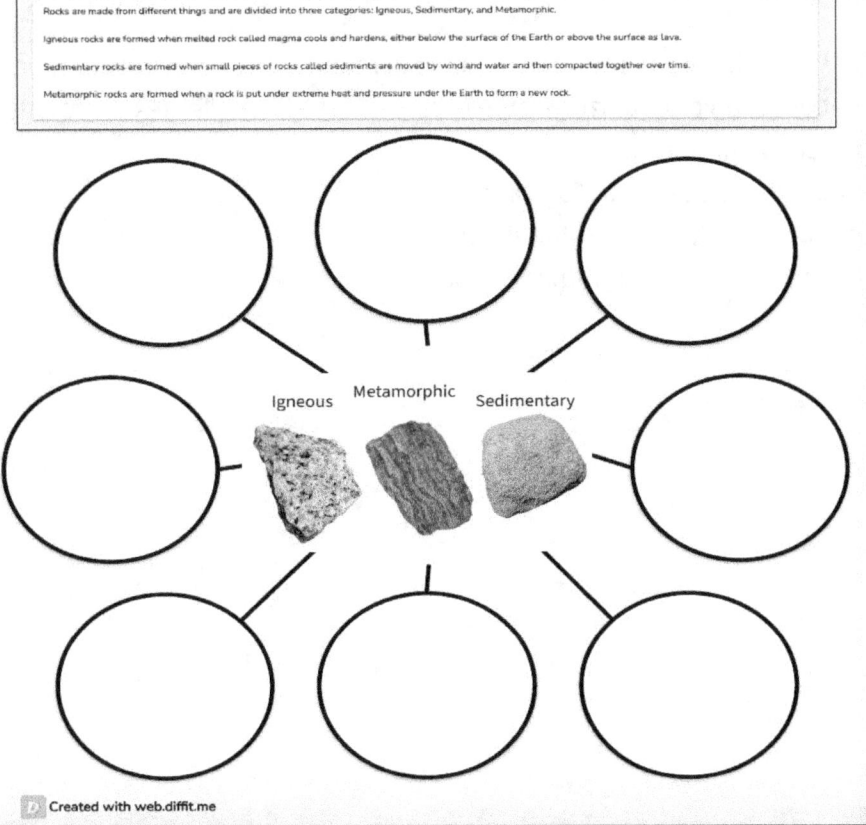

Bubble Map Graphic Organizer

Instructions: The center of the bubble map has an image that represents the reading to help get you started. Fill in the connecting bubbles with concepts, ideas, questions, and details that connect the image to the reading. Example: "This image connects to the reading because_____"

Reading Summary:

Rocks are made from different things and are divided into three categories: Igneous, Sedimentary, and Metamorphic.

Igneous rocks are formed when melted rock called magma cools and hardens, either below the surface of the Earth or above the surface as lava.

Sedimentary rocks are formed when small pieces of rocks called sediments are moved by wind and water and then compacted together over time.

Metamorphic rocks are formed when a rock is put under extreme heat and pressure under the Earth to form a new rock.

Igneous   Metamorphic   Sedimentary

Created with web.diffit.me

Pro Tips

Choose the Right Graphic Organizer

- **Identify Your Purpose**

    - **Organizing Info:** Venn diagram (compare/contrast), T-chart (two categories)
    - **Sequencing or process:** Flowchart or timeline for steps/events
    - **Cause and effect:** Cause-effect chart or chain of events
    - **Hierarchies and relationships:** Tree diagram or hierarchy chart
    - **Concept mapping:** Mind map or concept map for connecting ideas
    - **Problem-solving:** Decision tree or analysis chart

- **Match to Content**

    - **Simple comparisons:** T-charts or tables
    - **Complex ideas:** Concept maps or spider diagrams
    - **Chronological events:** Timelines or sequence charts

- **Consider Student Needs**

    - **Support zone:** Where the students need support to reach grade-level expectations (i.e. include in the graphic organizer simpler word choices, smaller text amounts, simpler grammatical structures)
    - **Visual learners:** Mind maps, web diagrams
    - **Step-by-step thinkers:** Flowcharts, timelines
    - **Comparative thinkers:** Venn diagrams, T-charts

StarTech—Your Digital Copilot

These tools can be used to create customized and leveled questions, helping educators provide differentiated instruction and ensuring that students are challenged at their appropriate learning levels.

- **Canva:** https://www.canva.com/
- **Gliffy:** https://www.gliffy.com/

The AI tools selected were free when researched.
AI evolves rapidly, so please verify before selecting and using.

 *Scan the QR code to access more Graphic Organizer examples.*

Cloze Activity

BOOST Move Breakdown

Boost Move	Definition	Why	When
Cloze Activity	An activity where students complete fill-in-the-blank sentences using words from a word bank to reinforce vocabulary and content	*Enhances vocabulary retention *Improves contextual understanding *Develops reading comprehension skills *Encourages active engagement *Provides immediate feedback *Adapts to all proficiency levels *Strengthens writing skills *Reinforces listening and speaking skills *Boosts confidence and fluency	*Practice *Review *Assessment *Reteach

Boost Move Specs

Cloze activities (fill-in-the-blank with a word bank) are like training grounds where MLs sharpen their vocabulary skills in a safe, supportive arena. After teaching new words, cloze challenges help students practice using them correctly, boosting both understanding and sentence-building power (Nation, 2013). This strengthens their meaning-making skills and trains them to stay locked in on the objective (Grabe & Stoller, 2019). It also gets them ready for bigger challenges like open-ended speaking and writing tasks (Schmitt, 2014).

Teachers can launch cloze activities at the end of a lesson as a quick checkpoint to assess understanding and give instant feedback. These mini-missions help teachers see what skills players have mastered and what areas still need practice (Richards & Rodgers, 2014). By reducing cognitive load and keeping the focus on meaning (Taylor, 1953; Gibbons, 2015), cloze challenges build confidence, helping learners wield new language skills with more precision and strength.

Step-by-Step Walkthrough

1. **Be Flexible**
   You can use the leveled text with simple meanings; small portions of leveled text; the leveled questions; or the vocabulary words and definitions to create your cloze activities.

2. **Leverage Technology**
   Remember, StarTech is your friend. You can create cloze activities and word banks for MLs at the beginner, intermediate and advanced levels in no time!

GAME MODE:
Real Classroom Examples

Grades 6–8

Word Bank	
study world	tested scientists

Science is the:

_____

of how the

_____

works

_____

_____

shared with

_____

Pro Tips

- The Cloze Activity can be integrated into both writing and speaking practice, helping students engage with the content in various ways.
- It can serve as a quiz or assessment after instruction, class discussions, small-group activities, practice sessions, review, learning stations, and reading assignments have been completed.
- Use color-coded sentences by level to help students self-select their challenge!

StarTech—Your Digital Copilot

These StarTech tools help streamline the creation of cloze activities, offering interactive, auto-graded, and customizable experiences for learners across different subjects and levels.

- **ReadTheory:** https://readtheory.org/
- **Liveworksheets:** https://www.liveworksheets.com/
- **Quizlet:** https://www.quizlet.com
- **Wordwall:** https://wordwall.net/
- **Blooket:** https://www.blooket.com/
- **Quizziz:** https://quizizz.com/
- **Kahoot!:** https://kahoot.com/
- **Rewordify:** https://rewordify.com/
- **Diffit:** https://web.diffit.me/
- **MagicSchoolAI:** https://www.magicschool.ai/

The AI tools selected were free when researched.
AI evolves rapidly, so please verify before selecting and using.

 **Scan the QR code to access the Cloze Template and examples.**

"Unlock the mystery! Cloze activities are like hidden quests— fill in the blanks to complete the story, gain new knowledge, and level up your language skills!"

Review Games

BOOST Move Breakdown

Boost Move	Definition	Why	When
Review Games	An engaging strategy that uses games with leveled review questions to reinforce content understanding in an interactive format. (Wright, Betteridge, & Buckby, 2006).	*Increases engagement and motivation *Reinforces vocabulary and content knowledge *Improves language retention through repetition *Lowers anxiety and creates a supportive learning environment *Encourages peer interaction and collaboration *Strengthens listening, speaking, reading, and writing skills *Provides immediate feedback for learning progress *Adapts to different proficiency levels and learning styles *Enhances problem-solving and critical thinking skills *Makes learning fun and memorable	*Practice *Review *Reteach

Boost Move Specs

Review games are like **bonus rounds** that help MLs practice vocabulary, grammar, and key concepts in a fun, low-pressure arena (Nation, 2013). Games build **player confidence**, especially for MLs who might feel anxious about challenges such as tests in a new language (Gibbons, 2015).

Review games also serve as **quick checkpoint scans** for teachers, offering instant insights into what players know and where they might need a few extra power-ups (Richards & Rodgers, 2014). Because games give **immediate feedback**, players can quickly spot what skills they've mastered and what needs more practice.

When classroom energy dips, a **fast-paced mini-game** can reengage learners and keep the environment dynamic, focused, and mission-ready (Schmitt, 2014). Review games are perfect for these instructional needs:

- **Transitions between topics**
- **Recharging player stamina**
- **Keeping every lesson active and moving**

Many review games turn learning into **co-op mode**, promoting the following:

- **Peer interaction**
- **Real-world communication** (negotiation, turn-taking, listening, etc.)
- **Academic and social language growth** (Gibbons, 2015)

Games often include **movement, visuals, and hands-on activities**, making the quests more concrete, memorable, and accessible for different player styles (Grabe & Stoller, 2019). They create opportunities for MLs to **use language in meaningful, action-packed ways**.

Having fun while learning **boosts memory**! When students enjoy the quest, their brains release "happy hormones" that help them **store and retrieve information faster**. Best of all, games **lower the affective filter** (Krashen, 1982), meaning players are less stressed and more willing to take risks, try new words, and build fluency—without fear. Games make learning active, exciting, and effective, and you'll watch your MLs' confidence and language skills soar!

Step-by-Step Walkthrough

1. Use leveled questions to play the game you choose.

GAME MODE:
Real Classroom Examples

There are so many fun games, so we have just suggested a few:

Find Your Partner Game

1. Give each student a card or sticky note. One card/note has a word, the other has the matching definition or picture.

2. Have students walk around the room. They read their card/note and listen to others.

3. Find the matches. Match word to definition, or word to picture.

4. Have students check with the teacher. Once students think they found a match, they show you to check.

5. Sit down together or cheer quietly. After finding their partner, they sit down or give a quiet celebration.

Review Relay Game

1. Divide the class into teams. Each team lines up in a row.

2. Give the first player a leveled question. It can be about vocabulary, a reading passage, or class content.

3. Have the student who answers the question, run to the back of the line. The next player gets a new question.

4. Keep going until all team members answer. Teams take turns until everyone has had a chance.

5. The first team to finish with correct answers wins!

Inside/Outside Circle Game

1. Make two circles. Half the class forms an inside circle, facing out. The other half forms an outside circle, facing in. Everyone has a partner.

2. Have students choose a paragraph from their leveled text to read.

3. Ask partners to take turns reading aloud. One student reads while the other listens, and then they switch.

4. Rotate. After both students read, the outside circle moves one person to the right. Students now have a new partner.

5. Repeat with new text or the same one. Keep going for a few rounds to build fluency.

Sports-Themed Review Game (Soccer/Baseball/Football)

1. Draw a soccer/baseball/football field on the board.

2. Make a soccer/baseball/football out of card stock, and put a magnet on the back.

3. Divide the class into teams.

4. Ask a leveled question-give the team two minutes to huddle together to discuss the answer.

5. Allow up to two minutes for one of the team members to give the answer. If correct, that team gets 1 point. If they get the answer wrong the other team has the chance to answer the question. If they get the right answer, they get 1 point.

6. Give the other team a chance to answer a leveled question.

7. After all the questions are answered, the team with the most points wins!

Board Game

1. Print the Board Game. Glue it inside a file folder.

2. Print the leveled questions from the leveled questions template. Have students cut them out into small squares.

3. Use colored beans or starbursts for each student's player piece.

4. Divide students into small groups. Each group will have a board game, dice, and leveled questions. Each student will have a player piece that is a different color.

5. Ask the first student to draw a question. If they answer the question correctly, they will roll the dice and move their piece that number of spaces.

6. Make sure each student has a turn.

7. The student who gets to the finish line first wins!

Pro Tips

- **Flexibility**: The board game is generic, meaning it can be reused across different themes or topics in learning stations or small groups.
- **Use review games to give students repeated, low-stress practice with math problems.**
- **Combine BOOST Moves:** Mix strategies. Add vocabulary and simple meanings to leveled questions for extra language practice.
- **Home Language Boost:** Let students collaborate in their home language during gameplay, then share answers in English to engage fully and build confidence.

StarTech—Your Digital Copilot

- This is your opportunity to use one of your StarTech tools provided to you by your school, district, or publisher of the curriculum you use.
- Become your own game master by creating your own game!

*Scan the QR code for a list
of Review Games and a game board template.*

Unleash your inner game designer! Using your imagination to create classroom games turns learning into an epic adventure where every student becomes a hero on their own quest for knowledge!

Reread Leveled Text

BOOST Move Breakdown

Boost Move	Definition	Why	When
Reread Leveled Text	A reading strategy that provides entire texts adapted to students' proficiency levels to build reading fluency and comprehension (Fountas & Pinnell, 2017).	*Reinforces vocabulary retention *Strengthens comprehension skills *Improves reading fluency and accuracy *Builds confidence in reading independently *Deepens understanding of text structure and meaning *Supports grammar and sentence pattern recognition *Encourages critical thinking and inferencing skills *Enhances automaticity in language processing *Bridges the gap to more complex texts *Helps MLs progress to the next proficiency level *Improves recall and long-term retention *Allows for deeper engagement with content *Helps identify new details and nuances in the text *Develops stamina for extended reading *Provides repeated exposure to academic language	*During teach *Reteach *Practice *Review

Boost Move Specs

Rereading leveled texts is like replaying a **mission with better gear**. Each pass builds stronger skills and unlocks deeper understanding. Rereading gives MLs a powerful way to **boost fluency, comprehension, and confidence** over time.

The **first read** is all about **decoding** and **recognizing new words,** like scouting the map and spotting key items (Samuels, 1979; Nation, 2013). **Subsequent reads** shift the focus to **building meaning, leveling up vocabulary**, and **boosting reading speed**, much like completing new objectives each time you replay a level (Vygotsky, 1978).

Every reread reinforces **vocabulary knowledge**, **sentence structure mastery**, and **critical thinking skills** (Schmitt, 2014; Grabe & Stoller, 2019). With each successful run, players grow stronger, moving faster through the text and thinking more strategically.

As MLs conquer rereading missions, they gain a real **sense of accomplishment**, **build self-efficacy**, and **develop the confidence** needed to tackle tougher quests ahead (Fountas & Pinnell, 2017; Dörnyei & Ushioda, 2021).

Rereading isn't just a repeat; it's a power-up!

Step-by-Step Walkthrough

Rereading isn't a one-size-fits-all move. It's a **flexible boost** that can be adapted to fit all kinds of quests and player needs. Just like in gaming, different missions call for different strategies!

Rereading might be used for these instructional purposes:

- After an initial run to clarify meaning
- Before tackling comprehension questions
- During vocabulary reviews to reinforce key words
- As prep for class discussions, writing tasks, or partner retells
- After a lesson to motivate MLs by demonstrating what they have accomplished

This mission can be activated in **small-group co-op mode**, flying **solo**, or **guided quests** with a teacher leading the way.

The steps you choose depend on the **mission goal**—whether you're building **fluency**, reinforcing **new language**, supporting **deeper comprehension**, or preparing players for assessments.

Because you can **adjust the strategy** based on proficiency levels and lesson goals, rereading stays one of the **most versatile tools in your BOOST arsenal**—ready to power up learning anytime, anywhere!

GAME MODE:
Real Classroom Examples

Activity Description:

This simple yet powerful activity uses a sheet protector and a highlighter to help MLs visually celebrate their reading progress. Place a clear sheet protector over a grade-level text. Provide each student with a dry-erase marker or highlighter. Have students reread a familiar passage and highlight or mark the words they can *now read and understand.*

Pro Tips

Below are games you can use with rereading.

1. **Fluency Relay**
   Students reread a sentence or paragraph aloud, passing it to the next partner or group. The goal is to maintain fluency and build confidence together.

2. **Read and Freeze**
   As students reread, call out "freeze!" randomly. The student must summarize what they just read or predict what comes next.

3. **Echo Reading Challenge**
   One student reads a sentence aloud; their partner echoes it with the same tone and expression—great for building fluency and intonation.

4. **Story Scramble**
   Cut a reread text into sentence strips. Students must work together to put the sentences back in the correct order.

5. **Partner Prediction**
   After a reread, partners take turns asking, "What do you think will happen next?" and give evidence from the text.

6. **Missing Word Mystery**
   Remove keywords from a reread passage. Students fill in the blanks using clues from the text to build vocabulary and comprehension.

7. **Reader's Theater**
   Turn the text into a short script. Students rehearse and perform it, building expression, fluency, and comprehension.

8. **Highlight Hunt**
   After rereading, students search for specific elements: new vocabulary, signal words, or parts of a sequence.

9. **Retell Relay**
   Teams take turns retelling parts of the text sentence by sentence. Each student adds to the retelling without repeating what was said.

10. **Comprehension Charades**
    After rereading, students act out events or vocabulary from the text, while others guess, playfully reinforcing key ideas.

StarTech—Your Digital Copilot

These tools help personalize reading experiences, enabling students to access content that matches their reading proficiency while ensuring they are challenged appropriately to grow their skills.

- **ReadTheory:** https://readtheory.org/
- **Quizlet:** https://www.quizlet.com
- **Wordwall:** https://wordwall.net/
- **Diffit:** https://web.diffit.me/

The AI tools selected were free when researched.
AI evolves rapidly, to please verify before selecting and using.

 **Scan the QR code for more rereading activities and ideas.**

"Replay the level! Rereading is like practicing your moves in a video game. Each time you get closer to perfection and ready to conquer the boss battle."

Conclusion

The BOOST Moves in this guide were created with one mission in mind: to empower multilingual learners *and* the amazing educators who support them every day. Born from real classrooms, global experiences, and a deep understanding of the time crunch teachers face, these strategies are practical, powerful, and ready to go.

Each BOOST Move is designed to help your students access grade-level content, grow in language proficiency, and gain the confidence they need to shine in science, math, history, and beyond. Whether your learners are just beginning their English journey or already soaring, these BOOST Moves can help them thrive.

Want to see how these strategies play out in real classrooms? Scan the QR codes in this book for ready-to-use examples across elementary, middle, and high school levels—designed to save you time and spark big results.

Be sure to visit our website, www.bestquesters.net for fresh Boost Moves, quick tips, downloadable resources, and new blog posts that keep your teaching energized. Don't miss our virtual and in-person workshops packed with practical ideas to support multilingual learners at every level. Be sure to follow us on social media for bonus Boosts, free sessions, and fun ways to connect with other educators on the same mission!

You've got the tools. You've got the heart. And now, you've got *The BOOST Playbook* to guide the way.

Let's open more doors, spark more joy, and build brighter futures—one BOOST Move at a time.

Appendix

STAR TECH TOOLS:
Our Artificial Intelligence Tips

Language models such as ChatGPT, Copilot, and Gemini offer powerful tools for supporting MLs in various aspects of language acquisition. By learning how to craft clear, targeted prompts, teachers can maximize the benefits of these models across multiple activities. This section explores suggestions to effectively prompt these models for some of our BOOST Moves, ensuring the responses are tailored to MLs' proficiency levels and needs.

By aligning prompts with instructional strategies and language levels, AI tools like ChatGPT can quickly create effective materials for multilingual learners. These best practices offer leveled prompts for each BOOST Move—beginning, intermediate, and advanced—making content accessible, vocabulary stronger, and learning more engaging. These examples demonstrate how easy it can be for you to generate customized, impactful resources that accelerate language growth and content understanding—with little prep time.

(The italicized words in parenthesis are instructions for the teacher, not part of the prompt.)

Prompt Suggestions for BOOST Moves for Beginner, Intermediate, and Advanced Level MLs.

BOOST Move	Beginner Level Prompt	Intermediate Level Prompt	Advanced Level Prompt
Leveled Text We recommend working backwards. By creating the leveled text first, it is easier to train your AI.	Create leveled text for beginner WIDA proficiency levels for *(fill in your grade level)* ___ grade MLs. For beginners, adapt the text with the smallest number of words possible and simple definitions. Put in bulleted format with simple 2–3 word sentences or phrases. *(Copy and paste your text)*	Create leveled text for intermediate WIDA proficiency levels for *(fill in your grade level)* ___ grade MLs. For intermediates, adapt the text with simple sentences, simple sentence structure, and simple definitions. *(Copy and paste your text)*	Create leveled text for advanced WIDA proficiency levels for *(fill in your grade level)*___grade MLs. For advanced learners, adapt the text by amplifying difficult words for MLs *(Add a list of words you feel will be difficult for advanced MLs that you want amplified.)* *(Copy and paste your text.)*
(Teacher: If you do not get the output you desire; add to or edit the prompt to get your desired results.)			

BOOST Move	Beginner Level Prompt	Intermediate Level Prompt	Advanced Level Prompt
Vocabulary	*(Cut and paste the beginner leveled text.)* *(Type this prompt.)* Create a table with the following headings: # Page # Word Translation Simple Meaning Picture= In the translation column, include both a _____translation and a _____ translation. (*Include the first languages of your MLs such as Spanish, Vietnamese, etc.*) Put the text in the left column and the simple definitions in the right column. *(Optional: You can add words you want them to include by typing 'MAKE SURE TO INCLUDE THESE WORDS AND SIMPLE DEFINITIONS.)* Include the simple definitions for the beginner WIDA proficiency levels.	*(Cut and paste the intermediate leveled text.)* *(Type this prompt.)* Create a table with the following headings: # Page # Word Translation Simple Meaning Picture= In the translation column, include both a _____translation and a _____ translation (*Include the first languages of your MLs such as Spanish, Vietnamese, etc.*) Put the text in the left column and the simple definitions in the right column. *(Optional: You can add words you want them to include by typing 'MAKE SURE TO INCLUDE THESE WORDS AND SIMPLE DEFINITIONS)*	*(Cut and paste the advanced leveled text.)* *(Type this prompt.)* Create a table with the following headings: # Page # Word Definition Put the text in the left column and the definitions in the right column. *(Optional: You can add words you want them to include by typing 'MAKE SURE TO INCLUDE THESE WORDS AND GRADE LEVEL DEFINITIONS FOR MLs at the (advanced) WIDA proficiency level.)* Include the grade-level definitions for the key terms in the text, academic language, and polysemous words.

BOOST Move	Beginner Level Prompt	Intermediate Level Prompt	Advanced Level Prompt
Vocabulary	Make the simple definitions very simple, using 1 or 2 words. *(You can ask them to add pictures.)* *(If the definitions are still too difficult you can give another prompt asking AI to simplify the definitions more.)*	Include the definitions for the intermediate WIDA proficiency levels. Make the simple definitions in simple sentences or phrases. *(If the definitions are still too difficult, you can give another prompt asking AI to simplify the definitions more.)*	*(If the definitions are still too difficult, you can give another prompt asking AI to simplify the definitions more.)*

(After you get the Vocabulary and Simple Meanings in AI, cut and paste the table into a Word Document and click on Table Design. Then Click the first table with gridlines.)

BOOST Move	Beginner Level Prompt	Intermediate Level Prompt	Advanced Level Prompt
Flashcards	Create a flashcard activity with a table, with the left column being the word and the right hand column being the definition of the word for the **beginner** WIDA proficiency level ML, recreate using 14 font, and make sure the definition cell is at least 1/2 an inch high. Make sure both columns are the same width.	Create a flashcard activity with a table, with the left column being the word and the right hand column being a definition of the word for the **intermediate** WIDA proficiency level ML, recreate using 14 font, and make sure the definition cell is at least 1/2 an inch high.	Create a flashcard activity with a table, with the left column being the word and the right hand column being a definition of the word for the **advanced** WIDA proficiency level ML, recreate using 14 font, and make sure the definition cell is at least 1/2 an inch high.

| Flashcards | Make it a downloadable Word version. *(Copy and paste the vocabulary and simple meanings table for the beginner into the prompt).* | Make sure both columns are the same width. Make it a downloadable Word version. *(Copy and paste the vocabulary and simple meanings table for the intermediate ML into the prompt).* | Make sure both columns are the same width. Make it a downloadable Word version. *(Copy and paste the vocabulary and definitions table for the advanced ML into the prompt).* |

(If you want the picture on the flashcard you can add this prompt: 'with a picture'
(You can copy the table and click on Table Design. Then click the first table with gridlines.)

BOOST Move	Beginner Level Prompt	Intermediate Level Prompt	Advanced Level Prompt
Matching	Create a matching activity for beginner MLs. List vocabulary words with numbers (1, 2, 3, etc.) on the left. On the right, list simple definitions without numbers. Students should match by writing the correct number of the word next to its definition. Use these vocabulary words: *(Copy and paste the vocabulary and simple meanings table for the beginner MLs into the prompt.)* Make it a downloadable Word version.	Create a matching activity for intermediate MLs. List vocabulary words with numbers (1, 2, 3, etc.) on the left. On the right, list simple definitions without numbers. Students should match by writing the correct number of the word next to its definition. Use these vocabulary words: *(Copy and paste the vocabulary and simple meanings table for the intermediate MLs into the prompt.)* Make it a downloadable Word version.	Create a matching activity for advanced MLs. List vocabulary words with numbers (1, 2, 3, etc.) on the left. On the right, list simple definitions without numbers. Students should match by writing the correct number of the word next to its definition. Use these vocabulary words: *(Copy and paste the vocabulary and definitions table for the advanced MLs into the prompt.)* Make it a downloadable Word version.

BOOST Move	Beginner Level Prompt	Intermediate Level Prompt	Advanced Level Prompt
Word Bank Quiz	Create a word bank activity with these instructions: where columns in table are 1st column #, 2nd column Simple Meaning, 3rd column Word from Word Bank. Use words from the beginner ML leveled text and vocabulary and simple meanings table.	Create a word bank activity with these instructions: where columns in table are 1st column #, 2nd column Simple Meaning, 3rd column Word from Word Bank. Use words from the intermediate ML leveled text and vocabulary and simple meanings table.	Create a word bank activity with these instructions: where columns in table are 1st column #, 2nd column Simple Meaning, 3rd column Word from Word Bank. Use words from the advanced ML leveled text and vocabulary and definitions table.

BOOST Move	Beginner Level Prompt	Intermediate Level Prompt	Advanced Level Prompt
Leveled Text with Simple Meanings	Create a leveled text with a simple definitions table using the beginner proficiency level text and vocabulary table with simple meanings. Put the text in the left column and the simple definitions in the right column. *(Copy and paste the vocabulary and simple meanings table for the beginner MLs into the prompt and the beginner leveled text.)* *(You can ask to add pictures.)*	Create a leveled text with a simple definitions table using the intermediate proficiency level text and vocabulary table with simple meanings. Put the text in the left column and the simple definitions in the right column. *(Copy and paste the vocabulary and simple meanings table for the intermediate MLs into the prompt and the intermediate leveled text.)*	Create a leveled text with a definitions table using the advanced proficiency level text and vocabulary table with definitions. Put the text on the left column and the definitions on the right column. *(Copy and paste the vocabulary and definitions table for the advanced MLs into the prompt and the advanced leveled text.)*
(Once the table is completed, you can copy and paste into Word.) *(You can copy the table and click on Table Design. Then click the first table with gridlines.)* *(You can also enlarge any pictures by highlighting the pictures and increase the size of the font.)*			

Getting Help and Staying Updated

If AI doesn't give you what you need right away, don't give up. Small changes to your prompt can make a big difference. For example, if a text AI produces is still too difficult for the ML, simply type "make the text simpler," and AI will do just that. And if you get stuck, we're here to help:

- Email us at info@bestquesters.net for direct support from our AI expert.
- Check our website for AI webinars, training, and updated tools.
- Visit often for new StarTech suggestions linked to each BOOST Move.

With AI-enhanced instruction, you're optimizing, customizing, and unlocking new levels of student engagement while saving your time and energy.

References Cited

Antioch University. "The Impact of Inclusive Education for English Language Learners." December 10, 2024. https://www.antioch.edu.

August, Diane, and Timothy Shanahan, eds. *Developing Literacy in Second-Language Learners: Report of the National Literacy Panel on Language-Minority Children and Youth.* New York: Routledge, 2017.

Aznan, N. A., and M. A. Saad. "The Use of Graphic Organiser on Second Language Students' Writing Performance." *IIUM Journal of Educational Studies* 11, no. 2 (2023): 115–137. https://www.researchgate.net/publication/376999583.

Bansal, Nidhi. 2023. *The Impact of Age on Second Language Acquisition: A Critical Review.* ResearchGate. https://www.researchgate.net/publication/384509951_The_impact_of_age_on_second_language_acquisition_a_critical_review.

Bloom, Benjamin S., ed. *Taxonomy of Educational Objectives: The Classification of Educational Goals. Handbook I: Cognitive Domain.* New York: David McKay Company, 1956.

Colorín Colorado. "Using Graphic Organizers with ELLs." Accessed 2024. https://www.colorincolorado.org/article/using-graphic-organizers-ells.

Comprehensive Center Network. *Strengthening the Multilingual Learner Teacher Pipeline Toolkit.* 2023. https://compcenternetwork.org/sites/default/files/ML-TeacherPipelineToolkit.pdf.

ChatGPT (OpenAI). "Editing Assistance on Proficiency Levels for Multilingual Learners." Accessed March 1, 2025. https://chat.openai.com/.

Dörnyei, Zoltán, and Ema Ushioda. *Teaching and Researching Motivation.* 3rd ed. London: Routledge, 2021.

Duke, Nell K., and P. David Pearson. "Effective Practices for Developing Reading Comprehension." *Journal of Research in Reading* 29, no. 2 (2002): 210–229. https://doi.org/10.1111/1467-9817.2002.00071.x.

Echevarria, Jana. "4 Ways to Integrate Language and Content." *Jana Echevarria Education Blog*, 2023. https://www.janaechevarria.com/?p=5398.

Echevarria, Jana, MaryEllen Vogt, and Deborah J. Short. *Making Content Comprehensible for English Learners: The SIOP Model.* 6th ed. Pearson, 2023.

Echevarría, Jana, MaryEllen Vogt, and Deborah J. Short. *Making Content Comprehensible for English Learners: The SIOP Model.* 5th ed. Pearson, 2017.

Education First. *Advancing Social and Emotional Learning for Multilingual Learners.* 2024. https://www.education-first.com/wp-content/uploads/2024/05/FINAL-Toward-Inclusivity-Advancing-Social-and-Emotional-Learning-for-Multilingual-Learners.pdf

Edutopia. "4 Practical Ways to Make Instruction Accessible for Multilingual Learners." *Edutopia*, 2021. https://www.edutopia.org/article/4-practical-ways-make-instruction-accessible-multilingual-learners/

Edutopia. "Teaching ELLs Content and English Simultaneously." *Edutopia*, 2024. https://www.edutopia.org/article/teaching-ells-content-english-simultaneously/

Ensemble Learning Group. *Challenges Multilingual Learners Face in U.S. Schools.* 2023. https://ensemblelearning.org/challenges-multilingual-learners-face

Fenner, Diane Staehr, Sydney Snyder, and Meghan Gregoire-Smith. *Unlocking Multilingual Learners' Potential: Strategies for Making Content Accessible.* 2nd ed. Thousand Oaks, CA: Corwin, 2024. https://www.corwin.com/books/unlocking-mls-potential-284441

Folse, Keith S. *Vocabulary Myths: Applying Second Language Research to Classroom Teaching.* Ann Arbor: University of Michigan Press, 2004.

Fountas, Irene C., and Gay Su Pinnell. *Guided Reading: Responsive Teaching Across the Grades.* Portsmouth, NH: Heinemann, 2016.

Freeman, David, and Meg Crawford. *Language and Cultural Barriers in U.S. Classrooms: Supporting Multilingual Learners.* New York: Routledge, 2023.

Freeman, David, and Yvonne Crawford. *Closing the Achievement Gap for ELLs: Using Culturally Responsive Teaching to Enhance Learning.* Thousand Oaks, CA: Corwin, 2023.

Gairns, Ruth, and Stuart Redman. *Working with Words: A Guide to Teaching and Learning Vocabulary.* Cambridge: Cambridge University Press, 1986.

Gándara, Patricia, and Russell Rumberger. "Challenges in Assessing English Learners' Academic Performance." *Educational Researcher* 53, no. 1 (2024): 15–28. https://journals.sagepub.com/doi/abs/10.3102/0013189X231215345

Gibbons, Pauline. *Scaffolding Language, Scaffolding Learning: Teaching English Language Learners in the Mainstream Classroom.* 2nd ed. Portsmouth, NH: Heinemann, 2015.

Grabe, William, and Fredricka L. Stoller. *Teaching and Researching Reading.* 3rd ed. London: Routledge, 2019.

Graves, Michael F. *The Vocabulary Book: Learning and Instruction.* New York: Teachers College Press, 2006.

Hansen-Thomas, Holly, Morgan Stewart, and Peyton Flint. "Addressing the Preparation Gap: Teacher Training for Multilingual Learners." *Journal of Teacher Education* 74, no. 2 (2023): 198–214. https://digitalcommons.unl.edu/cgi/viewcontent.cgi?article=1336&context=teachlearnfacpub.

Hartshorne, J. K., Tenenbaum, J. B., & Pinker, S. (2018). A critical period for second language acquisition: Evidence from 2/3 million English speakers. *Cognition, 177,* 263-277.

Hiver, Peter, et al. "Second Language Learning Through Play in Early Childhood Education: A Systematic Review." *Frontiers in Education,* 2024.

Huynh, Tan. "Making Assessments More Equitable for Multilingual Learners." *Edutopia,* July 28, 2023. https://www.edutopia.org/article/making-assessments-equitable-multilingual-students/.

Huynh, Thi. "Assessment Challenges for Multilingual Learners." *Journal of Educational Assessment* 15, no. 2 (2023): 123–135.

Jiang, Xuehui, and William Grabe. "Graphic Organizers in Reading Instruction: Research Findings and Issues." *Reading in a Foreign Language* 19, no. 1 (2007): 34–55.

Kerekes, Judit, et al. "Cultural Barriers in the Classroom: Strategies for Inclusion." *International Journal of Multicultural Education* 23, no. 1 (2021): 45–60.

Kerekes, Julie, Shakina Rajendram, Mama Adjetey-Nii Owoo, and Yiran Zhang. "Teachers' Takes on Supporting Multilingual Learners in K-12 Classrooms." *Journal of Multilingual Education Research* 11, no. 1 (2021): 4–20. https://files.eric.ed.gov/fulltext/EJ1340537.pdf.

Kondal, B. *Developing Speaking Skills through Task-Based Materials for the Second Language Learners*. Scholars' Press, 2017.

Krashen, S. D. *Principles and Practice in Second Language Acquisition*. Pergamon Press, 1982.

Krashen, Stephen D. *Second Language Acquisition and Second Language Learning*. Oxford: Pergamon Press, 1981.

Language Magazine. "Breaking Down the Monolingual Wall VIII: Our Students Are Multilingual—Shouldn't Assessment Be?" *Language Magazine*, September 17, 2024.

Language Magazine. "Rethinking Assessments for Multilingual Learners." *Language Magazine*, April 2024.

Learning Policy Institute. *Long-Term English Learners in California*. December 2024. https://learningpolicyinstitute.org/product/ca-long-term-english-learners-report.

Learning Policy Institute. "Long-Term English Learners: Challenges and Solutions." 2024.

Levinson, R., and K. Cooke. "U.S. Teachers Face Language Barriers, Student Trauma as Record Migration Reaches Classrooms." *Reuters*, October 5, 2024.

Li, Ping, and Heisoo Jeong. "The Social Brain of Language: Grounding Second Language Learning in Social Interaction." *NPJ Science of Learning* 5 (2020): 8. https://doi.org/10.1038/s41539-020-0068-7.

Li Wei, and Ofelia García. "Not a First Language but One Repertoire: Translanguaging as a Decolonizing Project." *RELC Journal* (2022).

Lichtman, Karen. "Age and Learning Environment: Are Children Implicit Second Language Learners?" *Journal of Child Language* 43, no. 2 (2016): 457–84.

Provides evidence that children primarily use implicit mechanisms—such as distributional pattern recognition—to acquire grammar, rather than explicit instruction

López, Fabiola, Maria Esteban-Guitart, and Lisa Garcia. "Preparing Educators for Multilingual Classrooms: A Global Perspective." *Frontiers in Education* 9 (2024): 1–15.

https://www.frontiersin.org/journals/education/articles/10.3389/fed-uc.2024.1282936/full.

López, F., Patricia Gándara, and M. Hopkins. "Challenges in Teacher Preparation for English Learners." *Educational Policy Review*, 2024.

Marzano, Robert J. *Building Academic Vocabulary: Teacher's Manual.* Alexandria, VA: ASCD, 2004.

Marzano, Robert J. *Building Background Knowledge for Academic Achievement: Research on What Works in Schools.* Alexandria, VA: Association for Supervision and Curriculum Development, 2004.

McAllister, John. "The Burden of Differentiation: How Teachers Manage Workload When Supporting English Learners." *ERIC Journal of Education Policy*, 2022. https://files.eric.ed.gov/fulltext/EJ1340537.pdf.

Menken, Kate, and Tatyana Kleyn. *The Long-Term Impact of English Learner Labeling: Evidence from New York City.* New York: Routledge, 2012.

Menken, Kate, and Tatyana Kleyn. "Spotlight on 'Long-Term English Language Learners': Characteristics and Prior Schooling Experiences of an Invisible Population." *Teaching for Biliteracy*, 2012. https://www.teachingforbiliteracy.com/wp-content/uploads/2014/09/menken-kleyn-chae-2012-secondary-students.pdf.

Mitchell, Corey. "Recruiting More Bilingual Teachers: The Challenges and Solutions." *Education Week*, September 2023. https://www.edweek.org/teaching-learning/recruiting-more-bilingual-teachers-the-challenges-and-solutions/2023/09.

Nation, I. S. P. *Learning Vocabulary in Another Language.* Cambridge: Cambridge University Press, 2001.

Newport, Elissa L. "Maturational Constraints on Language Learning." *Cognitive Science* 14, no. 1 (1990): 11–28.

Nutta, J. W., C. Strebel, F. M. Mihai, E. Crevecoeur-Bryant, and K. Mokhtari. *Show, Tell, Build: Twenty Key Instructional Tools for Educating English Learners.* Cambridge, MA: Harvard Education Press, 2018.

Nutta, J. W., C. Strebel, K. Mokhtari, F. Mihai, and E. Crevecoeur-Bryant. *Educating English Learners: What Every Classroom Teacher Needs to Know.* 2nd ed. Cambridge, MA: Harvard Education Press, 2020.

Nutta, Joyce, Kouider Mokhtari, and Carine Strebel. *Preparing Every Teacher to Reach English Learners: A Practical Guide for Teacher Educators*. Cambridge, MA: Harvard Education Press, 2020.

Ortega, Lourdes. *Understanding Second Language Acquisition*. 2nd ed. New York: Routledge, 2014.

Rice Kinder Institute. "Factors Contributing to Long-Term English Learner Status." *Kinder Institute for Urban Research*. Accessed 2022.

Rice Kinder Institute for Urban Research. "Long-Term English Learners (LTELs): What Factors Are Associated with the Likelihood of an English Learner Becoming a Long-Term English Learner?" *Kinder Institute for Urban Research*, May 2022. https://kinder.rice.edu/research/what-factors-are-associated-likelihood-english-learner-becoming-long-term-english-learner.

Richards, Jack C., and Theodore S. Rodgers. *Approaches and Methods in Language Teaching*. 3rd ed. Cambridge: Cambridge University Press, 2014.

Rodriguez, Ana, and Ravi Patel. "Trauma-Informed Practices for Supporting MLs in the Classroom." *Journal of Multicultural Education* 18, no. 3 (2024): 112–129.

Rodriguez, J. L., and R. Rodríguez. "An Evaluation of the Effectiveness of the Use of Graphic Organizers and ELLs' Academic Performance." *Journal of Educational Research and Practice* 10, no. 1 (2020): 1–15. https://eric.ed.gov/?id=ED643047.

Rodriguez, Lilia, and Ananya Patel. "Addressing Trauma in Multilingual Classrooms: Strategies for Teachers." *Reuters*, October 5, 2024. https://www.reuters.com/world/us/us-teachers-face-language-barriers-student-trauma-record-migration-reaches-2024-10-05.

SAGE Publications. *Issues in Assessment for Multilingual Learners*. SAGE Publications, 2024. https://us.sagepub.com/sites/default/files/upm-assets/129762_book_item_129762.pdf.

Salerno, April S., and Amanda K. Kibler. "Supporting English Learners in the Middle: Culturally Responsive and Sustaining Practices to Support Student Identity Development and Sense of Belonging." *Middle School Journal* 51, no. 2 (2020): 24–32. https://www.amle.org/research/supporting-english-learners-in-the-middle-culturally-responsive-and-sustaining-practices-to-support-student-identity-development-and-sense-of-belonging/.

Salgado, R. M., P. S. Koike, R. Maglasang, and J. Minoza. "Overcoming Linguistic and Cultural Barriers in English Language Learning: An Exploration of Culturally Responsive Pedagogy." *The English Teacher* 53, no. 2 (2024): 91–108. https://www.researchgate.net/publication/384965524_Overcoming_Linguistic_and_Cultural_Barriers_in_English_Language_Learning_An_Exploration_of_Culturally_Responsive_Pedagogy.

Samuels, S. Jay. "The Method of Repeated Readings." *The Reading Teacher* 32, no. 4 (1979): 403–408.

Schleppegrell, Mary J. *The Language of Schooling: A Functional Linguistics Perspective.* Mahwah, NJ: Lawrence Erlbaum Associates, 2004.

Schmitt, Norbert. "Review Article: Instructed Second Language Vocabulary Learning." *Language Teaching Research* 12, no. 3 (2008): 329–363. https://doi.org/10.1177/1362168808089921.

Schmitt, Norbert. *Vocabulary in Language Teaching.* 2nd ed. Cambridge: Cambridge University Press, 2014.

Schwartz, J., and M. Bone. *Retelling, Reliving, and Reflecting: Strategies for Developing Comprehension and Language Experiences.* Portsmouth, NH: Heinemann, 1995.

Schwartz, Robert M., and Mary F. Bone. *Retrospective Miscue Analysis: An Overview.* Urbana, IL: National Council of Teachers of English, 1995.

Silverman, Rebecca D., and Anna M. Hartranft. *Developing Vocabulary and Oral Language in Young Children.* New York: Guilford Press, 2015.

SupportEd. "Unlocking Multilingual Learners' Potential." *SupportEd Resources,* 2025. https://supported.com/unlocking-mls/.

Taylor & Francis Online. "Emotional Challenges of Teaching Multilingual Learners: A Review." *Journal of Education Research* 45, no. 4 (2024): 78–91.

Taylor & Francis Online. "Teacher Emotions in Teaching Multilingual Students." *Taylor & Francis Online,* 2024. https://think.taylorandfrancis.com/special_issues/teacher-emotions-teaching-multilingual-students/.

Taylor, Wilson L. "Cloze Procedure: A New Tool for Measuring Readability." *Journalism Quarterly* 30, no. 4 (1953): 415–433.

U.S. Department of Education. *Providing Effective Supports for English Learners in K–12 Schools.* Washington, DC: U.S. Department of Education, 2022.

https://www.ed.gov/news/press-releases/us-department-education-releases-new-guidance-support-english-learners.

Villegas, Malia. "Accountability for Long-Term English Learners." *Kappan Online*, September 2023. https://kappanonline.org/accountability-for-english-learners-villegas/.

Vygotsky, L. S. *Mind in Society: The Development of Higher Psychological Processes*. Cambridge, MA: Harvard University Press, 1978.

WCER (Wisconsin Center for Education Research). "Examining Statewide LTEL Trends and Their Educational Impact." *WCER Report*, 2024. https://wcer.wisc.edu/news/detail/first-extensive-study-of-long-term-english-learners-finds-significant-diffe.

WestEd. "Focusing Formative Assessment on the Needs of English Language Learners." *WestEd*, 2024. https://www.wested.org/resource/focusing-formative-assessment-on-the-needs-of-english-language-learners/.

WestEd. "Reevaluating Assessments for MLs: Best Practices and Policy Recommendations." *WestEd Reports*, 2024.

WIDA. *WIDA English Language Development Standards Framework, 2020 Edition: Kindergarten–Grade 12*. Madison, WI: Board of Regents of the University of Wisconsin System, 2020.

WIDA. "Trauma-Informed Considerations and Strategies for Multilingual Learners." *WIDA Focus Bulletin*, 2023. https://wida.wisc.edu/sites/default/files/resource/FocusBulletin-Trauma-Informed-Considerations-Strategies-Multilingual-Learners.pdf.

Wright, Andrew, David Betteridge, and Michael Buckby. *Games for Language Learning*. 3rd ed. Cambridge: Cambridge University Press, 2006.

Zadina, Janet N. *Multiple Pathways to the Student Brain: Energizing and Enhancing Instruction*. San Francisco: Jossey-Bass, 2014.

Zwiers, Jeff. *Building Academic Language: Meeting Common Core Standards Across Disciplines*. San Francisco, CA: Jossey-Bass, 2014.

About the Authors

Donita Grissom, PhD

Dr. Donita Grissom's journey in education is a testament to her passion for teaching, empowering others, and fostering meaningful connections. Her path has been marked by dedication, expertise, and an unwavering commitment to equipping educators with the skills and knowledge to transform lives. With degrees from Southeast Missouri State University, the University of Florida, and a Ph.D. in TESOL from the University of Central Florida, Donita has shaped the field of multilingual education and teacher training, mentoring future leaders as the Ed.D. TESOL Specialization Advisor. Her research on Snyder's *hope theory* influenced a desire to support English learners facing trauma and has made her a sought-after keynote speaker, hope specialist, and life coach. As an English Specialist for the US State Department, she champions global collaboration, bridging cultures through language and education. Beyond academia, she is a mentor, professional consultant, and devoted mother and grandmother, embodying the true essence of an educator—one who not only imparts knowledge but also inspires hope, resilience, and transformation in others.

If you're looking for an inspiring keynote speaker, a dynamic professional development workshop, or expert coaching and mentoring for your team, Dr. Donita Grissom brings a wealth of knowledge, passion, and real-world experience to the Best Quester's team. As a specialist in multilingual education, teacher training, and hope theory, she empowers educators, leaders, and organizations with practical strategies to foster raising hope levels, reduce stress, increase resilience, and overall thriving in well-being. The Best Questers team delivers impactful sessions tailored to your needs. To schedule an event or discuss collaboration opportunities, contact **info@bestquesters.net**.

Debbie Simões, MEd

A unique ability to see potential beyond circumstances enables Debbie to turn stumbling blocks into stepping stones, empowering educators to bridge the gap between potential and performance. Inspired by a college professor who introduced her to leaders such as Zig Ziglar and John Maxwell, she knew early on that teaching and inspiring others was her calling. Despite a brain injury that prevented her from completing student teaching as an undergrad, she went on to earn an MEd from Arizona State University and another from the University of Maryland.

As an educator in Phoenix, Washington, DC, and South Florida, Debbie saw firsthand the urgent need to equip educators with the skills to cultivate vibrant, connected learning communities where happiness and high achievement are an everyday reality. She's navigated the complexities of education as a teacher, principal, and director of a university lab school, equipping her with the insights to empower young scholars and educators at every level. She is a Nationally Certified Trainer with the Center for Teacher Effectiveness, a Maxwell Leadership Certified Speaker, Trainer, and Coach, and a certified life and business coach with a heart to add value to others. In 2021, she founded Best Questers to skyrocket teacher retention and student achievement through dynamic, data-backed professional development that helps teachers and students love stepping into their greatness together every day. When she's not out Best-Questing, Debbie enjoys her South Florida garden sanctuary with Mr. Fabulous (her husband), their yellow lab, Buddy, and the fab four felines.

Are you ready to say yes to the practical, outside-the-box solutions you've been missing—higher teacher retention, student attendance, motivation, achievement? Say no to the same old struggles, costly curriculums, and band-aid fixes that don't move the needle.

Debbie is available to provide professional development to help build the future your school or district deserves! Available for get-up-and-go keynotes, retreats, professional learning, team building, group coaching and community building! She offers "Time to Teach Classroom Leadership Workshops" to deliver proactive strategies to predict and prevent problem behaviors, maintain self- control, and preserve the integrity of instruction (available for college credit). To schedule an event or discuss collaboration opportunities, contact **info@bestquesters.net**.

Amy England-Aglio, EdS

Amy is an educator and instructional designer with more than 18 years of experience across online, blended, and in-person settings. A passionate advocate for teacher development and student-centered learning, she is known for pioneering brain-based instructional models and mentoring educators through data-driven coaching. Her workshops and professional learning have supported thousands of teachers and students in inclusive excellence, second language acquisition, project-based learning, AI integration, and culturally responsive teaching.

Amy has designed upper-level world language curricula, taught Spanish and ESOL, built open-source online courses, and trained educators in both K–12 and higher education. While teaching full-time in a digital high school, she created practical tools—including live discussion-based assessments (DBAs), peer-collaboration models, and personalized coaching systems—and developed websites and digital learning tools to enhance accessibility and engagement.

Beyond the classroom, Amy co-founded the Golden Keys Foundation, a nonprofit that empowers educators through mini-grants and passion projects. She is co-owner of Best Questers, which creates innovative learning adventures for educators and students, and owner of Ladybug Mobile & Wedding Services, providing notary, document support, virtual assistance, and wedding officiation for the Central Florida community.

She holds an Education Specialist (Ed.S.) in Curriculum & Instruction (Educational Leadership) from Stetson University; an M.Ed. in Instructional Technology from Nova Southeastern University; a Bachelor of Business Studies from the University of Technology Sydney; and a Bachelor of International Business (Honors) from the University of Lincoln, where she earned the Dean's Award and Best First-Year Student recognition.

The BOOST Playbook reflects Amy's belief in equity, empowerment, and sustainable growth—for educators and the students they serve.

Leslie Mendez, PhD

Dr. Leslie Mendez's career reflects her passion for education, multilingual learning, and empowering others to thrive through knowledge and connection. With an Ed.D. in Curriculum and Instruction with a TESOL specialty from the University of Central Florida, she has dedicated her career to advancing multilingual education and teacher preparation. Dr. Mendez has led large-scale federal grants such as Project MELTS, securing national recognition for pioneering digital badging and micro-credentialing systems that transformed teacher development for English learners.

Her work spans K–12, higher education, healthcare, and corporate training, where she has consistently brought innovation, strategic solutions, and cross-industry collaboration to complex challenges. She has co-authored publications on multilingual teacher education, instructional technology, and equity in learning, and presented at leading national and international conferences including TESOL International and AACTE.

As an instructional designer, consultant, and trainer, Dr. Mendez specializes in multilingual education, curriculum design, and performance optimization, equipping educators and organizations with tools to foster resilience, equity, and meaningful impact. Beyond her professional roles, she embodies the spirit of an agent of change—committed to helping others succeed, thrive, and lead with vision.

www.ingramcontent.com/pod-product-compliance
Lightning Source LLC
Chambersburg PA
CBHW081536120626
46550CB00009B/2752